THE EXTRAORDIN...

OF

ARSÈNE LUPIN

GENTLEMAN-BURGLAR

BY

MAURICE LEBLANC

———

Translated from the French
By GEORGE MOREHEAD

———

M. A. DONOHUE & CO.
CHICAGO

CONTENTS

ARSÈNE LUPIN
Gentleman - Burglar

CHAPTER I

THE ARREST OF ARSÈNE LUPIN

IT was a strange ending to a voyage
that had commenced in a most aus-
picious manner. The transatlantic
steamship *La Provence* was a swift and comfortable vessel, under the command of a most
affable man. The passengers constituted a
select and delightful society. The charm of
new acquaintances and improvised amuse-
ments served to make the time pass agree-
ably. We enjoyed the pleasant sensation of
being separated from the world, living, as it
were, upon an unknown island, and consequently obliged to be sociable with each other.

Have you ever stopped to consider how
much originality and spontaneity emanate
from these various individuals who, on the

preceding evening, did not even know each
other, and who are now, for several days, con-
demned to lead a life of extreme intimacy,
jointly defying the anger of the ocean, the terrible onslaught of the waves, the violence of
the tempest and the agonizing monotony of
the calm and sleepy water? Such a life becomes a sort of tragic existence, with its
storms and its grandeurs, its monotony and
its diversity; and that is why, perhaps, we
embark upon that short voyage with mingled
feelings of pleasure and fear.

But, during the past few years, a new sensation has been added to the life of the transatlantic traveler. The little floating island
is now attached to the world from which it
was once quite free. A bond unites them, even
in the very heart of the watery wastes of the
Atlantic. That bond is the wireless telegraph,
by means of which we receive news in the
most mysterious manner. We know full well
that the message is not transported by the
medium of a hollow wire. No, the mystery
is even more inexplicable, more romantic,
and we must have recourse to the wings of
the air in order to explain this new miracle.
During the first day of the voyage, we felt
that we were followed, escorted, preceded

even, by that distant voice, which, from time
to time, whispered to one of us a few words
from the receding world. Two friends spoke
to me. Ten, twenty others sent gay or sombre
words of parting to other passengers.

On the second day, at a distance of five
hundred miles from the French coast, in the
midst of a violent storm, we received the following message by means of the wireless
telegraph:

"Arsène Lupin is on your vessel, first
cabin, blonde hair, wound right fore-arm,
travelling alone under name of R........"

At that moment, a terrible flash of light-
ning rent the stormy skies. The electric
waves were interrupted. The remainder of
the despatch never reached us. Of the name
under which Arsène Lupin was concealing
himself, we knew only the initial.

If the news had been of some other character, I have no doubt that the secret would
have been carefully guarded by the tele-
graphic operator as well as by the officers of
the vessel. But it was one of those events
calculated to escape from the most rigorous
discretion. The same day, no one knew how,
the incident became a matter of current gos-
sip and every passenger was aware that the

famous Arsène Lupin was hiding in our midst.

Arsène Lupin in our midst! the irrepressible burglar whose exploits had been narrated in all the newspapers during the past few months! the mysterious individual with whom Ganimard, our shrewdest detective, had been engaged in an implacable conflict amidst interesting and picturesque surroundings. Arsène Lupin, the eccentric gentleman who operates only in the châteaux and salons, and who, one night, entered the residence of Baron Schormann, but emerged empty-handed, leaving, however, his card on which he had scribbled these words: "Arsène Lupin, gentleman-burglar, will return when the furniture is genuine." Arsène Lupin, the man of a thousand disguises: in turn a chauffeur, detective, bookmaker, Russian physician, Spanish bull-fighter, commercial traveler, robust youth, or decrepit old man.

Then consider this startling situation: Arsène Lupin was wandering about within the limited bounds of a transatlantic steamer; in that very small corner of the world, in that dining saloon, in that smoking room, in that music room! Arsène Lupin was, perhaps, this gentleman....or that one....my neigh-

bor at the table....the sharer of my stateroom....

"And this condition of affairs will last for
five days!" exclaimed Miss Nelly Underdown, next morning. "It is unbearable! I
hope he will be arrested."

Then, addressing me, she added:

"And you, Monsieur d'Andrézy, you are
on intimate terms with the captain; surely
you know something?"

I should have been delighted had I possessed any information that would interest
Miss Nelly. She was one of those magnificent creatures who inevitably attract attention in every assembly. Wealth and beauty
form an irresistible combination, and Nelly
possessed both.

Educated in Paris under the care of a
French mother, she was now going to visit
her father, the millionaire Underdown of
Chicago. She was accompanied by one of
her friends, Lady Jerland.

At first, I had decided to open a flirtation
with her; but, in the rapidly growing intimacy of the voyage, I was soon impressed by
her charming manner and my feelings became too deep and reverential for a mere flirtation. Moreover, she accepted my attentions

with a certain degree of favor. She con-
descended to laugh at my witticisms and
display an interest in my stories. Yet I felt
that I had a rival in the person of a young
man with quiet and refined tastes; and it
struck me, at times, that she preferred his
taciturn humor to my Parisian frivolity. He
formed one in the circle of admirers that surrounded Miss Nelly at the time she addressed
to me the foregoing question. We were all
comfortably seated in our deck-chairs. The
storm of the preceding evening had cleared
the sky. The weather was now delightful.

"I have no definite knowledge, mademoiselle," I replied, "but can not we, ourselves,
investigate the mystery quite as well as the
detective Ganimard, the personal enemy of
Arsène Lupin?"

"Oh! oh! you are progressing very fast,
monsieur."

"Not at all, mademoiselle. In the first
place, let me ask, do you find the problem a
complicated one?"

"Very complicated."

"Have you forgotten the key we hold for
the solution of the problem?"

"What key?"

"In the first place, Lupin calls himself Monsieur R——."

"Rather vague information," she replied.

"Secondly, he is traveling alone."

"Does that help you?" she asked.

"Thirdly, he is blonde."

"Well?"

"Then we have only to peruse the passenger-list, and proceed by the process of elimination."

I had that list in my pocket. I took it out and glanced through it. Then I remarked:

"I find that there are only thirteen men on the passenger-list whose names begin with the letter R."

"Only thirteen?"

"Yes, in the first cabin. And of those thirteen, I find that nine of them are accompanied by women, children or servants. That leaves only four who are travelling alone. First, the Marquis de Raverdan——"

"Secretary to the American Ambassador," interrupted Miss Nelly. "I know him."

"Major Rawson," I continued.

"He is my uncle," some one said.

"Mon. Rivolta."

"Here!" exclaimed an Italian, whose face was concealed beneath a heavy black beard.

Miss Nelly burst into laughter, and exclaimed: "That gentleman can scarcely be called a blonde."

"Very well, then," I said, "we are forced to the conclusion that the guilty party is the last one on the list."

"What is his name?"

"Mon. Rozaine. Does anyone know him?"

No one answered. But Miss Nelly turned to the taciturn young man, whose attentions to her had annoyed me, and said:

"Well, Monsieur Rozaine, why do you not answer?"

All eyes were now turned upon him. He was a blonde. I must confess that I myself felt a shock of surprise, and the profound silence that followed her question indicated that the others present also viewed the situation with a feeling of sudden alarm. However, the idea was an absurd one, because the gentleman in question presented an air of the most perfect innocence.

"Why do I not answer?" he said. "Because, considering my name, my position as a solitary traveler and the color of my hair, I have already reached the same conclusion, and now think that I should be arrested."

He presented a strange appearance as he

uttered these words. His thin lips were
drawn closer than usual and his face was
ghastly pale, whilst his eyes were streaked
with blood. Of course, he was joking, yet
his appearance and attitude impressed us
strangely.

"But you have not the wound?" said Miss
Nelly, naïvely.

"That is true," he replied, "I lack the
wound."

Then he pulled up his sleeve, removing his
cuff, and showed us his arm. But that action
did not deceive me. He had shown us his left
arm, and I was on the point of calling his attention to the fact, when another incident di-
verted our attention. Lady Jerland, Miss
Nelly's friend, came running towards us in a
state of great excitement, exclaiming:

"My jewels, my pearls! Some one has
stolen them all!"

No, they were not all gone, as we soon
found out. The thief had taken only part of
them; a very curious thing. Of the diamond
sunbursts, jewelled pendants, bracelets and
necklaces, the thief had taken, not the largest
but the finest and most valuable stones. The
mountings were lying upon the table. I saw
them there, despoiled of their jewels, like

flowers from which the beautiful colored
petals had been ruthlessly plucked. And this
theft must have been committed at the time
Lady Jerland was taking her tea; in broad
daylight, in a stateroom opening on a much
frequented corridor; moreover, the thief had
been obliged to force open the door of the
stateroom, search for the jewel-case, which
was hidden at the bottom of a hat-box, open
it, select his booty and remove it from the
mountings.

Of course, all the passengers instantly
reached the same conclusion; it was the work
of Arsène Lupin.

That day, at the dinner table, the seats to
the right and left of Rozaine remained vacant; and, during the evening, it was ru-
mored that the captain had placed him under
arrest, which information produced a feeling
of safety and relief. We breathed once more.
That evening, we resumed our games and
dances. Miss Nelly, especially, displayed a
spirit of thoughtless gayety which convinced
me that if Rozaine's attentions had been
agreeable to her in the beginning, she had
already forgotten them. Her charm and
good-humor completed my conquest. At midnight, under a bright moon, I declared my

devotion with an ardor that did not seem to
displease her.

But, next day, to our general amazement,
Rozaine was at liberty. We learned that the
evidence against him was not sufficient. He
had produced documents that were perfectly
regular, which showed that he was the son
of a wealthy merchant of Bordeaux. Besides,
his arms did not bear the slightest trace of
a wound.

"Documents! Certificates of birth!" exclaimed the enemies of Rozaine, "of course,
Arsène Lupin will furnish you as many as
you desire. And as to the wound, he never
had it, or he has removed it."

Then it was proven that, at the time of the
theft, Rozaine was promenading on the deck.
To which fact, his enemies replied that a man
like Arsène Lupin could commit a crime without being actually present. And then, apart
from all other circumstances, there remained
one point which even the most skeptical could
not answer: Who except Rozaine, was travelling alone, was a blonde, and bore a name
beginning with R? To whom did the telegram point, if it were not Rozaine?

And when Rozaine, a few minutes before
breakfast, came boldly toward our group,

Miss Nelly and Lady Jerland arose and
walked away.

An hour later, a manuscript circular was
passed from hand to hand amongst the sail-
ors, the stewards, and the passengers of all
classes. It announced that Mon. Louis Rozaine offered a reward of ten thousand francs
for the discovery of Arsène Lupin or other
person in possession of the stolen jewels.

"And if no one assists me, I will unmask
the scoundrel myself," declared Rozaine.

Rozaine against Arsène Lupin, or rather
according to current opinion, Arsène Lupin
himself against Arsène Lupin; the contest
promised to be interesting.

Nothing developed during the next two
days. We saw Rozaine wandering about,
day and night, searching, questioning, investigating. The captain, also, displayed com-
mendable activity. He caused the vessel to
be searched from stem to stern; ransacked
every stateroom under the plausible theory
that the jewels might be concealed anywhere
except in the thief's own room.

"I suppose they will find out something
soon," remarked Miss Nelly to me. "He may
be a wizard, but he cannot make the diamonds
and pearls become invisible."

"Certainly not," I replied, "but he should examine the lining of our hats and vests and everything we carry with us."

Then, exhibiting my kodak, a 9x12 with which I had been photographing her in various poses, I added: "In an apparatus no larger than that, a person could hide all of Lady Jerland's jewels. He could pretend to take pictures and no one would suspect the game."

"But I have heard it said that every thief leaves some clue behind him."

"That may be generally true, I replied, "but there is one exception: Arsène Lupin."

"Why?"

"Because he concentrates his thoughts not only on the theft, but on all the circumstances connected with it that could serve as a clue to his identity."

"A few days ago, you were more confident."

"Yes, but since then I have seen him at work."

"And what do you think about it now?" she asked.

"Well, in my opinion, we are wasting our time."

And, as a matter of fact, the investigation

had produced no result. But, in the meantime, the captain's watch had been stolen.
He was furious. He quickened his efforts
and watched Rozaine more closely than before. But, on the following day, the watch
was found in the second officer's collar-box.

This incident caused considerable astonishment, and displayed the humorous side of
Arsène Lupin, burglar though he was, but
dilettante as well. He combined business
with pleasure. He reminded us of the author
who almost died in a fit of laughter provoked
by his own play. Certainly, he was an artist
in his peculiar line of work, and whenever
I saw Rozaine, gloomy and reserved, and
thought of the double rôle that he was playing, I accorded him a certain measure of admiration.

On the following evening, the officer on
deck duty heard groans emanating from the
darkest corner of the ship. He approached
and found a man lying there, his head enveloped in a thick gray scarf and his hands tied
together with a heavy cord. It was Rozaine.
He had been assaulted, thrown down and
robbed. A card, pinned to his coat, bore
these words: "Arsène Lupin accepts with
pleasure the ten thousand francs offered by

Mon. Rozaine." As a matter of fact, the stolen pocket-book contained twenty thousand francs.

Of course, some accused the unfortunate man of having simulated this attack on himself. But, apart from the fact that he could not have bound himself in that manner, it was established that the writing on the card was entirely different from that of Rozaine, but, on the contrary, resembled the handwriting of Arsène Lupin as it was reproduced in an old newspaper found on board.

Thus it appeared that Rozaine was not Arsène Lupin; but was Rozaine, the son of a Bordeaux merchant. And the presence of Arsène Lupin was once more affirmed, and that in a most alarming manner.

Such was the state of terror amongst the passengers that none would remain alone in a stateroom or wander singly in unfrequented parts of the vessel. We clung together as a matter of safety. And yet the most intimate acquaintances were estranged by a mutual feeling of distrust. Arsène Lupin was, now, anybody and everybody. Our excited imaginations attributed to him miraculous and unlimited power. We supposed him capable of assuming the most unexpected disguises; of being, by turns, the highly respectable Major Rawson or the noble Marquis de Raverdan, or even—for we no longer stopped with the accusing letter R—or even such or such a person well known to all of us, and having wife, children and servants.

The first wireless despatches from America brought no news; at least, the captain did not communicate any to us. The silence was not reassuring.

Our last day on the steamer seemed interminable. We lived in constant fear of some disaster. This time, it would not be a simple theft or a comparatively harmless assault; it would be a crime, a murder. No one imagined that Arsène Lupin would confine himself to those two trifling offences. Absolute master of the ship, the authorities powerless, he could do whatever he pleased; our property and lives were at his mercy.

Yet those were delightful hours for me, since they secured to me the confidence of Miss Nelly. Deeply moved by those startling events and being of a highly nervous nature, she spontaneously sought at my side a protection and security that I was pleased to give her. Inwardly, I blessed Arsène Lupin. Had he not been the means of bringing me

and Miss Nelly closer to each other? Thanks
to him, I could now indulge in delicious
dreams of love and happiness—dreams that,
I felt, were not unwelcome to Miss Nelly. Her
smiling eyes authorized me to make them;
the softness of her voice bade me hope.

As we approached the American shore, the
active search for the thief was apparently
abandoned, and we were anxiously awaiting
the supreme moment in which the mysterious
enigma would be explained. Who was Arsène Lupin? Under what name, under what
disguise was the famous Arsène Lupin concealing himself? And, at last, that supreme
moment arrived. If I live one hundred years,
I shall not forget the slightest detail of it.

"How pale you are, Miss Nelly," I said to
my companion, as she leaned upon my arm,
almost fainting.

"And you!" she replied, "ah! you are so
changed."

"Just think! this is a most exciting moment, and I am delighted to spend it with
you, Miss Nelly. I hope that your memory
will sometimes revert——"

But she was not listening. She was nervous and excited. The gangway was placed
in position, but, before we could use it, the

uniformed customs officers came on board.
Miss Nelly murmured:

"I shouldn't be surprised to hear that Arsène Lupin escaped from the vessel during
the voyage."

"Perhaps he preferred death to dishonor,
and plunged into the Atlantic rather than be
arrested."

"Oh, do not laugh," she said.

Suddenly I started, and, in answer to her
question, I said:

"Do you see that little old man standing at
the bottom of the gangway?"

"With an umbrella and an olive-green
coat?"

"It is Ganimard."

"Ganimard?"

"Yes, the celebrated detective who has
sworn to capture Arsène Lupin. Ah! I can
understand now why we did not receive any
news from this side of the Atlantic. Ganimard was here! and he always keeps his business secret."

"Then you think he will arrest Arsène
Lupin?"

"Who can tell? The unexpected always
happens when Arsène Lupin is concerned in
the affair."

"Oh!" she exclaimed, with that morbid curiosity peculiar to women, "I should like to see him arrested."

"You will have to be patient. No doubt, Arsène Lupin has already seen his enemy and will not be in a hurry to leave the steamer."

The passengers were now leaving the steamer. Leaning on his umbrella, with an air of careless indifference, Ganimard appeared to be paying no attention to the crowd that was hurrying down the gangway. The Marquis de Raverdan, Major Rawson, the Italian Rivolta, and many others had already left the vessel when Rozaine appeared. Poor Rozaine!

"Perhaps it is he, after all," said Miss Nelly to me. "What do you think?"

"I think it would be very interesting to have Ganimard and Rozaine in the same picture. You take the camera. I am loaded down."

I gave her the camera, but too late for her to use it. Rozaine was already passing the detective. An American officer, standing behind Ganimard, leaned forward and whispered in his ear. The French detective shrugged his shoulders and Rozaine passed on. Then, my God, who was Arsène Lupin?

"Yes," said Miss Nelly, aloud, "who can it be?"

Not more than twenty people now remained on board. She scrutinized them one by one, fearful that Arsène Lupin was not amongst them.

"We cannot wait much longer," I said to her.

She started toward the gangway. I followed. But we had not taken ten steps when Ganimard barred our passage.

"Well, what is it?" I exclaimed.

"One moment, monsieur. What's your hurry?"

"I am escorting mademoiselle."

"One moment," he repeated, in a tone of authority. Then, gazing into my eyes, he said:

"Arsène Lupin, is it not?"

I laughed, and replied: "No, simply Bernard d'Andrezy."

"Bernard d'Andrezy died in Macedonia three years ago."

"If Bernard d'Andrezy were dead, I should not be here. But you are mistaken. Here are my papers."

"They are his; and I can tell you exactly how they came into your possession."

"You are a fool!" I exclaimed. "Arsène Lupin sailed under the name of R——"

"Yes, another of your tricks; a false scent that deceived them at Havre. You play a good game, my boy, but this time luck is against you."

I hesitated a moment. Then he hit me a sharp blow on the right arm, which caused me to utter a cry of pain. He had struck the wound, yet unhealed, referred to in the telegram.

I was obliged to surrender. There was no alternative. I turned to Miss Nelly, who had heard everything. Our eyes met; then she glanced at the kodak I had placed in her hands, and made a gesture that conveyed to me the impression that she understood everything. Yes, there, between the narrow folds of black leather, in the hollow centre of the small object that I had taken the precaution to place in her hands before Ganimard arrested me, it was there I had deposited Rozaine's twenty thousand francs and Lady Jerland's pearls and diamonds.

Oh! I pledge my oath that, at that solemn moment, when I was in the grasp of Ganimard and his two assistants, I was perfectly indifferent to everything, to my arrest, the

hostility of the people, everything except this
one question: what will Miss Nelly do with
the things I had confided to her?

In the absence of that material and conclu-
sive proof, I had nothing to fear; but would
Miss Nelly decide to furnish that proof?
Would she betray me? Would she act the
part of an enemy who cannot forgive, or that
of a woman whose scorn is softened by feelings of indulgence and involuntary sympathy?

She passed in front of me. I said nothing,
but bowed very low. Mingled with the other
passengers, she advanced to the gangway
with my kodak in her hand. It occurred to
me that she would not dare to expose me pub-
licly, but she might do so when she reached a
more private place. However, when she had
passed only a few feet down the gangway,
with a movement of simulated awkwardness,
she let the camera fall into the water between
the vessel and the pier. Then she walked
down the gangway, and was quickly lost to
sight in the crowd. She had passed out of
my life forever.

For a moment, I stood motionless. Then,
to Ganimard's great astonishment, I muttered:

"What a pity that I am not an honest man!"

Such was the story of his arrest as narrated to me by Arsène Lupin himself. The various incidents, which I shall record in writing at a later day, have established between us certain ties....shall I say of friendship? Yes, I venture to believe that Arsène Lupin honors me with his friendship, and that it is through friendship that he occasionally calls on me, and brings, into the silence of my library, his youthful exuberance of spirits, the contagion of his enthusiasm, and the mirth of a man for whom destiny has naught but favors and smiles.

His portrait? How can I describe him? I have seen him twenty times and each time he was a different person; even he himself said to me on one occasion: "I no longer know who I am. I cannot recognize myself in the mirror." Certainly, he was a great actor, and possessed a marvelous faculty for disguising himself. Without the slightest effort, he could adopt the voice, gestures and mannerisms of another person.

"Why," said he, "why should I retain a definite form and feature? Why not avoid the danger of a personality that is ever the same? My actions will serve to identify me.''

Then he added, with a touch of pride:

''So much the better if no one can ever say with absolute certainty: There is Arsène Lupin! The essential point is that the public may be able to refer to my work and say, without fear of mistake: Arsène Lupin did that!

CHAPTER II

ARSÈNE LUPIN IN PRISON

HERE is no tourist worthy of the name who does not know the banks of the Seine, and has not noticed, in passing, the little feudal castle of the Malaquis, built upon a rock in the centre of the river. An arched bridge connects it with the shore. All around it, the calm waters of the great river play peacefully amongst the reeds, and the wagtails flutter over the moist crests of the stones.

The history of the Malaquis castle is stormy like its name, harsh like its outlines. It has passed through a long series of combats, sieges, assaults, rapines and massacres. A recital of the crimes that have been committed there would cause the stoutest heart to tremble. There are many mysterious legends connected with the castle, and they tell us of a famous subterranean tunnel that formerly led to the abbey of Jumieges and to the manor of Agnes Sorel, mistress of Charles VII.

In that ancient habitation of heroes and
brigands, the Baron Nathan Cahorn now
lived; or Baron Satan as he was formerly
called on the Bourse, where he had acquired
a fortune with incredible rapidity. The lords
of Malaquis, absolutely ruined, had been
obliged to sell the ancient castle at a great
sacrifice. It contained an admirable collection of furniture, pictures, wood carvings
and faience. The Baron lived there alone,
attended by three old servants. No one ever
enters the place. No one had ever beheld the
three Rubens that he possessed, his two Watteau, his Jean Goujon pulpit, and the many
other treasures that he had acquired by a
vast expenditure of money at public sales.

Baron Satan lived in constant fear, not for
himself, but for the treasures that he had accumulated with such an earnest devotion and
with so much perspicacity that the shrewdest
merchant could not say that the Baron had
ever erred in his taste or judgment. He loved
them—his bibelots. He loved them intensely,
like a miser; jealously, like a lover. Every
day, at sunset, the iron gates at either end of
the bridge and at the entrance to the court of
honor are closed and barred. At the least

touch on these gates, electric bells will ring throughout the castle.

One Thursday in September, a letter-carrier presented himself at the gate at the head of the bridge, and, as usual, it was the Baron himself who partially opened the heavy portal. He scrutinized the man as minutely as if he were a stranger, although the honest face and twinkling eyes of the postman had been familiar to the Baron for many years. The man laughed, as he said:

"It is only I, Monsieur le Baron. It is not another man wearing my cap and blouse."

"One can never tell," muttered the Baron.

The man handed him a number of newspapers, and then said:

"And now, Monsieur le Baron, here is something new."

"Something new?"

"Yes, a letter. A registered letter."

Living as a recluse, without friends or business relations, the baron never received any letters, and the one now presented to him immediately aroused within him a feeling of suspicion and distrust. It was like an evil omen. Who was this mysterious correspondent that dared to disturb the tranquillity of his retreat?

"You must sign for it, Monsieur le Baron."

He signed; then took the letter, waited
until the postman had disappeared beyond
the bend in the road, and, after walking nervously to and fro for a few minutes, he
leaned against the parapet of the bridge and
opened the envelope. It contained a sheet of
paper, bearing this heading: Prison de la
Santé, Paris. He looked at the signature:
Arsène Lupin. Then he read:

"Monsieur le Baron:

"There is, in the gallery in your castle, a
picture of Philippe de Champaigne, of exquisite finish, which pleases me beyond
measure. Your Rubens are also to my taste,
as well as your smallest Watteau. In the
salon to the right, I have noticed the Louis
XIII cadence-table, the tapestries of Beau-
vais, the Empire gueridon signed 'Jacob,'
and the Renaissance chest. In the salon to
the left, all the cabinet full of jewels and
miniatures.

"For the present, I will content myself
with those articles that can be conveniently
removed. I will therefore ask you to pack
them carefully and ship them to me, charges
prepaid, to the station at Batignolles, within
eight days, otherwise I shall be obliged to

remove them myself during the night of 27 September; but, under those circumstances, I shall not content myself with the articles above mentioned.

"Accept my apologies for any inconvenience I may cause you, and believe me to be your humble servant,

"Arsène Lupin."

"P. S.—Please do not send the largest Watteau. Although you paid thirty thousand francs for it, it is only a copy, the original having been burned, under the Directoire by Barras, during a night of debauchery. Consult the memoirs of Garat.

"I do not care for the Louis XV châtelaine, as I doubt its authenticity."

That letter completely upset the baron. Had it borne any other signature, he would have been greatly alarmed—but signed by Arsène Lupin!

As an habitual reader of the newspapers, he was versed in the history of recent crimes, and was therefore well acquainted with the exploits of the mysterious burglar. Of course, he knew that Lupin had been arrested in America by his enemy Ganimard and was at present incarcerated in the Prison de la Santé. But he knew also that any miracle

might be expected from Arsène Lupin. Moreover, that exact knowledge of the castle, the
location of the pictures and furniture, gave
the affair an alarming aspect. How could he
have acquired that information concerning
things that no one had ever seen?

The baron raised his eyes and contem-
plated the stern outlines of the castle, its
steep rocky pedestal, the depth of the sur-
rounding water, and shrugged his shoulders.
Certainly, there was no danger. No one in
the world could force an entrance to the sanc-
tuary that contained his priceless treasures.

No one, perhaps, but Arsène Lupin! For
him, gates, walls and drawbridges did not
exist. What use were the most formidable
obstacles or the most careful precautions, if
Arsène Lupin had decided to effect an entrance?

That evening, he wrote to the Procurer of
the Republique at Rouen. He enclosed the
threatening letter and solicited aid and protection.

The reply came at once to the effect that
Arsène Lupin was in custody in the Prison
de la Santé, under close surveillance, with no
opportunity to write such a letter, which was,
no doubt, the work of some impostor. But,

as an act of precaution, the Procurer had
submitted the letter to an expert in handwriting, who declared that, in spite of certain re-
semblances, the writing was not that of the
prisoner.

But the words "in spite of certain re-
semblances" caught the attention of the
baron; in them, he read the possibility of a
doubt which appeared to him quite sufficient
to warrant the intervention of the law. His
fears increased. He read Lupin's letter over
and over again. "I shall be obliged to remove them myself." And then there was the
fixed date: the night of 27 September.

To confide in his servants was a proceeding repugnant to his nature; but now, for the
first time in many years, he experienced the
necessity of seeking counsel with some one.
Abandoned by the legal official of his own dis-
trict, and feeling unable to defend himself
with his own resources, he was on the point
of going to Paris to engage the services of a
detective.

Two days passed; on the third day, he was
filled with hope and joy as he read the following item in the *Réveil de Caudebec*, a newspaper published in a neighboring town:

"We have the pleasure of entertaining in

our city, at the present time, the veteran detective Mon. Ganimard who acquired a world-wide reputation by his clever capture of Arsène Lupin. He has come here for rest and recreation, and, being an enthusiastic fisherman, he threatens to capture all the fish in our river.''

Ganimard! Ah, here is the assistance desired by Baron Cahorn! Who could baffle the schemes of Arsène Lupin better than Ganimard, the patient and astute detective? He was the man for the place.

The baron did not hesitate. The town of Caudebec was only six kilometres from the castle, a short distance to a man whose step was accelerated by the hope of safety.

After several fruitless attempts to ascertain the detective's address, the baron visited the office of the *Réveil*, situated on the quai. There he found the writer of the article who, approaching the window, exclaimed:

''Ganimard? Why, you are sure to see him somewhere on the quai with his fishing-pole. I met him there and chanced to read his name engraved on his rod. Ah, there he is now, under the trees.''

''That little man, wearing a straw hat?''

"Exactly. He is a gruff fellow, with little to say."

Five minutes later, the baron approached the celebrated Ganimard, introduced himself, and sought to commence a conversation, but that was a failure. Then he broached the real object of his interview, and briefly stated his case. The other listened, motionless, with his attention riveted on his fishing-rod. When the baron had finished his story, the fisherman turned, with an air of profound pity, and said:

"Monsieur, it is not customary for thieves to warn people they are about to rob. Arsène Lupin, especially, would not commit such a folly."

"But——"

"Monsieur, if I had the least doubt, believe me, the pleasure of again capturing Arsène Lupin would place me at your disposal. But, unfortunately, that young man is already under lock and key."

"He may have escaped."

"No one ever escaped from the Santé."

"But, he——"

"He, no more than any other."

"Yet——"

"Well, if he escapes, so much the better.

I will catch him again. Meanwhile, you go home and sleep soundly. That will do for the present. You frighten the fish.''

The conversation was ended. The baron returned to the castle, reassured to some extent by Ganimard's indifference. He examined the bolts, watched the servants, and, during the next forty-eight hours, he became almost persuaded that his fears were groundless. Certainly, as Ganimard had said, thieves do not warn people they are about to rob.

The fateful day was close at hand. It was now the twenty-sixth of September and nothing had happened. But at three o'clock the bell rang. A boy brought this telegram:

''No goods at Batignolles station. Prepare everything for to-morrow night. Arsène.''

This telegram threw the baron into such a state of excitement that he even considered the advisability of yielding to Lupin's demands.

However, he hastened to Caudebec. Ganimard was fishing at the same place, seated on a campstool. Without a word, he handed him the telegram.

''Well, what of it?'' said the detective.

''What of it? But it is to-morrow.''

"What is to-morrow?"

"The robbery! The pillage of my collections!"

Ganimard laid down his fishing-rod, turned to the baron, and exclaimed, in a tone of impatience:

"Ah! Do you think I am going to bother myself about such a silly story as that!"

"How much do you ask to pass to-morrow night in the castle?"

"Not a sou. Now, leave me alone."

"Name your own price. I am rich and can pay it."

This offer disconcerted Ganimard, who replied, calmly:

"I am here on a vacation. I have no right to undertake such work."

"No one will know. I promise to keep it secret."

"Oh! nothing will happen."

"Come! three thousand francs. Will that be enough?"

The detective, after a moment's reflection, said:

"Very well. But I must warn you that you are throwing your money out of the window."

"I do not care."

"In that case....but, after all, what do we
know about this devil Lupin! He may have
quite a numerous band of robbers with him.
Are you sure of your servants?"

"My faith——"

"Better not count on them. I will telegraph for two of my men to help me. And
now, go! It is better for us not to be seen
together. To-morrow evening about nine
o'clock."

    *   *   *   *   *

The following day—the date fixed by Arsène Lupin—Baron Cahorn arranged all his
panoply of war, furbished his weapons, and,
like a sentinel, paced to and fro in front of the
castle. He saw nothing, heard nothing. At
half-past eight o'clock in the evening, he dismissed his servants. They occupied rooms in
a wing of the building, in a retired spot, well
removed from the main portion of the castle.
Shortly thereafter, the baron heard the sound
of approaching footsteps. It was Ganimard
and his two assistants—great, powerful fellows with immense hands, and necks like
bulls. After asking a few questions relating
to the location of the various entrances and
rooms, Ganimard carefully closed and barricaded all the doors and windows through

which one could gain access to the threatened rooms. He inspected the walls, raised the tapestries, and finally installed his assistants in the central gallery which was located between the two salons.

"No nonsense! We are not here to sleep. At the slightest sound, open the windows of the court and call me. Pay attention also to the water-side. Ten metres of perpendicular rock is no obstacle to those devils."

Ganimard locked his assistants in the gallery, carried away the keys, and said to the baron:

"And now, to our post."

He had chosen for himself a small room located in the thick outer wall, between the two principal doors, and which, in former years, had been the watchman's quarters. A peep-hole opened upon the bridge; another on the court. In one corner, there was an opening to a tunnel.

"I believe you told me, Monsieur le Baron, that this tunnel is the only subterranean entrance to the castle and that it has been closed up from time immemorial?"

"Yes."

"Then, unless there is some other entrance, known only to Arsène Lupin, we are quite safe.''

He placed three chairs together, stretched himself upon them, lighted his pipe and sighed:

''Really, Monsieur le Baron, I feel ashamed to accept your money for such a sinecure as this. I will tell the story to my friend Lupin. He will enjoy it immensely.''

The baron did not laugh. He was anxiously listening, but heard nothing save the beating of his own heart. From time to time, he leaned over the tunnel and cast a fearful eye into its depths. He heard the clock strike eleven, twelve, one.

Suddenly, he seized Ganimard's arm. The latter leaped up, awakened from his sleep.

''Do you hear?'' asked the baron, in a whisper.

''Yes.''

''What is it?''

''I was snoring, I suppose.''

''No, no, listen.''

''Ah! yes, it is the horn of an automobile.''

''Well?''

''Well! it is very improbable that Lupin would use an automobile like a battering-ram to demolish your castle. Come, Monsieur le

Baron, return to your post. I am going to sleep. Good-night.''

That was the only alarm. Ganimard resumed his interrupted slumbers, and the baron heard nothing except the regular snoring of his companion. At break of day, they left the room. The castle was enveloped in a profound calm; it was a peaceful dawn on the bosom of a tranquil river. They mounted the stairs, Cahorn radiant with joy, Ganimard calm as usual. ' They heard no sound; they saw nothing to arouse suspicion.

"What did I tell you, Monsieur le Baron? Really, I should not have accepted your offer. I am ashamed.''

He unlocked the door and entered the gallery. Upon two chairs, with drooping heads and pendent arms, the detective's two assistants were asleep.

"Tonnerre de nom d'un chien!'' exclaimed Ganimard. At the same moment, the baron cried out:

"The pictures! The credence!''

He stammered, choked, with arms outstretched toward the empty places, toward the denuded walls where naught remained but the useless nails and cords. The Watteau, disappeared! The Rubens, carried

away! The tapestries taken down! The
cabinets, despoiled of their jewels!

"And my Louis XVI candelabra! And the
Regent chandelier!....And my twelfth-cen-
tury Virgin!"

He ran from one spot to another in wildest
despair. He recalled the purchase price of
each article, added up the figures, counted
his losses, pell-mell, in confused words and
unfinished phrases. He stamped with rage;
he groaned with grief. He acted like a ruined
man whose only hope is suicide.

If anything could have consoled him, it
would have been the stupefaction displayed
by Ganimard. The famous detective did not
move. He appeared to be petrified; he examined the room in a listless manner. The windows?....closed. The locks on the doors?
....intact. Not a break in the ceiling; not a
hole in the floor. Everything was in perfect order. The theft had been carried out
methodically, according to a logical and in-
exorable plan.

"Arsène Lupin....Arsène Lupin," he
muttered.

Suddenly, as if moved by anger, he rushed
upon his two assistants and shook them vio-
lently. They did not awaken.

"The devil!" he cried. "Can it be possible?"

He leaned over them and, in turn, examined them closely. They were asleep; but their repose was unnatural.

"They have been drugged," he said to the baron.

"By whom?"

"By him, of course, or his men under his direction. The work bears his stamp."

"In that case, I am lost—nothing can be done."

"Nothing," assented Ganimard.

"It is dreadful; it is monstrous."

"Lodge a complaint."

"What good will that do?"

"Oh; it is well to try it. The law has some resources."

"The law! Bah! it is useless. You represent the law, and, at this moment, when you should be looking for a clue and trying to discover something, you do not even stir."

"Discover something with Arsène Lupin! Why, my dear monsieur, Arsène Lupin never leaves any clue behind him. He leaves nothing to chance. Sometimes I think he put himself in my way and simply allowed me to arrest him in America."

"Then, I must renounce my pictures! He has taken the gems of my collection. I would give a fortune to recover them. If there is no other way, let him name his own price."

Ganimard regarded the baron attentively, as he said:

"Now, that is sensible. Will you stick to it?"

"Yes, yes. But why?"

"An idea that I have."

"What is it?"

"We will discuss it later—if the official examination does not succeed. But, not one word about me, if you wish my assistance."

He added, between his teeth:

"It is true I have nothing to boast of in this affair."

The two assistants were gradually regaining consciousness with the bewildered air of people who come out of an hypnotic sleep. They opened their eyes and looked about them in astonishment. Ganimard questioned them; they remembered nothing.

"But you must have seen some one?"

"No."

"Can't you remember?"

"No, no."

"Did you drink anything?"

They considered a moment, and then one of them replied:

"Yes, I drank a little water."

"Out of that carafe?"

"Yes."

"So did I," declared the other.

Ganimard smelled and tasted it. It had no particular taste and no odor.

"Come," he said, "we are wasting time here. One can't decide an Arsène Lupin problem in five minutes. But, morbleu! I swear I will catch him again."

The same day, a charge of burglary was duly preferred by Baron Cahorn against Arsène Lupin, a prisoner in the Prison de la Santé.

*   *   *   *   *

The baron afterwards regretted making the charge against Lupin when he saw his castle delivered over to the gendarmes, the procureur, the judge d'instruction, the newspaper reporters and photographers, and a throng of idle curiosity-seekers.

The affair soon became a topic of general discussion, and the name of Arsène Lupin excited the public imagination to such an extent that the newspapers filled their columns with the most fantastic stories of his exploits which found ready credence amongst their readers.

But the letter of Arsène Lupin that was published in the *Echo de France* (no one ever knew how the newspaper obtained it), that letter in which Baron Cahorn was impudently warned of the coming theft, caused considerable excitement. The most fabulous theories were advanced. Some recalled the existence of the famous subterranean tunnels, and that was the line of research pursued by the officers of the law, who searched the house from top to bottom, questioned every stone, studied the wainscoting and the chimneys, the window-frames and the girders in the ceilings. By the light of torches, they examined the immense cellars where the lords of Malaquis were wont to store their munitions and provisions. They sounded the rocky foundation to its very centre. But it was all in vain. They discovered no trace of a subterranean tunnel. No secret passage existed.

But the eager public declared that the pictures and furniture could not vanish like so many ghosts. They are substantial, material things and require doors and windows for their exits and their entrances, and so do the people that remove them. Who were those people? How did they gain access to the castle? And how did they leave it?

The police officers of Rouen, convinced of their own impotence, solicited the assistance of the Parisian detective force. Mon. Dudouis, chief of the Sûreté, sent the best sleuths of the iron brigade. He himself spent forty-eight hours at the castle, but met with no success. Then he sent for Ganimard, whose past services had proved so useful when all else failed.

Ganimard listened, in silence, to the instructions of his superior; then, shaking his head, he said:

"In my opinion, it is useless to ransack the castle. The solution of the problem lies elsewhere."

"Where, then?"

"With Arsène Lupin."

"With Arsène Lupin! To support that theory, we must admit his intervention."

"I do admit it. In fact, I consider it quite certain."

"Come, Ganimard, that is absurd. Arsène Lupin is in prison."

"I grant you that Arsène Lupin is in prison, closely guarded; but he must have fetters on his feet, manacles on his wrists, and a gag in his mouth before I change my opinion.''

''Why so obstinate, Ganimard?''

''Because Arsène Lupin is the only man in France of sufficient calibre to invent and carry out a scheme of that magnitude.''

''Mere words, Ganimard.''

''But true ones. Look! What are they doing? Searching for subterranean passages, stones swinging on pivots, and other nonsense of that kind. But Lupin doesn't employ such old-fashioned methods. He is a modern cracksman, right up to date.''

''And how would you proceed?''

''I should ask your permission to spend an hour with him.''

''In his cell?''

''Yes. During the return trip from America we became very friendly, and I venture to say that if he can give me any information without compromising himself he will not hesitate to save me from incurring useless trouble.''

It was shortly after noon when Ganimard entered the cell of Arsène Lupin. The latter, who was lying on his bed, raised his head and uttered a cry of apparent joy.

"Ah! This is a real surprise. My dear Ganimard, here!"

"Ganimard himself."

"In my chosen retreat, I have felt a desire for many things, but my fondest wish was to receive you here."

"Very kind of you, I am sure."

"Not at all. You know I hold you in the highest regard."

"I am proud of it."

"I have always said: Ganimard is our best detective. He is almost,—you see how candid I am!—he is almost as clever as Sherlock Holmes. But I am sorry that I cannot offer you anything better than this hard stool. And no refreshments! Not even a glass of beer! Of course, you will excuse me, as I am here only temporarily."

Ganimard smiled, and accepted the proffered seat. Then the prisoner continued:

"Mon Dieu, how pleased I am to see the face of an honest man. I am so tired of those devils of spies who come here ten times a day to ransack my pockets and my cell to satisfy themselves that I am not preparing to escape. The government is very solicitous on my account."

"It is quite right."

"Why so? I should be quite contented if they would allow me to live in my own quiet way."

"On other people's money."

"Quite so. That would be so simple. But here, I am joking, and you are, no doubt, in a hurry. So let us come to business, Ganimard. To what do I owe the honor of this visit?"

"The Cahorn affair," declared Ganimard, frankly.

"Ah! Wait, one moment. You see I have had so many affairs! First, let me fix in my mind the circumstances of this particular case....Ah! yes, now I have it. The Cahorn affair, Malaquis castle, Seine-Inférieure.... Two Rubens, a Watteau, and a few trifling articles."

"Trifling!"

"Oh! ma foi, all that is of slight importance. But it suffices to know that the affair interests you. How can I serve you, Ganimard?"

"Must I explain to you what steps the authorities have taken in the matter?"

"Not at all. I have read the newspapers and I will frankly state that you have made very little progress."

"And that is the reason I have come to see you."

"I am entirely at your service."

"In the first place, the Cahorn affair was managed by you?"

"From A to Z."

"The letter of warning? the telegram?"

"All mine. I ought to have the receipts somewhere."

Arsène opened the drawer of a small table of plain white wood which, with the bed and stool, constituted all the furniture in his cell, and took therefrom two scraps of paper which he handed to Ganimard.

"Ah!" exclaimed the detective, in surprise, "I thought you were closely guarded and searched, and I find that you read the newspapers and collect postal receipts."

"Bah! these people are so stupid! They open the lining of my vest, they examine the soles of my shoes, they sound the walls of my cell, but they never imagine that Arsène Lupin would be foolish enough to choose such a simple hiding-place."

Ganimard laughed, as he said:

"What a droll fellow you are! Really, you bewilder me. But, come now, tell me about the Cahorn affair."

"Oh! oh! not quite so fast! You would rob me of all my secrets; expose all my little tricks. That is a very serious matter."

"Was I wrong to count on your complaisance?"

"No, Ganimard, and since you insist——"

Arsène Lupin paced his cell two or three times, then, stopping before Ganimard, he asked:

"What do you think of my letter to the baron?"

"I think you were amusing yourself by playing to the gallery."

"Ah! playing to the gallery! Come, Ganimard, I thought you knew me better. Do I, Arsène Lupin, ever waste my time on such puerilities? Would I have written that letter if I could have robbed the baron without writing to him? I want you to understand that that letter was indispensable; it was the motor that set the whole machine in motion. Now, let us discuss together a scheme for the robbery of the Malaquis castle. Are you willing?"

"Yes, proceed."

"Well, let us suppose a castle carefully closed and barricaded like that of the Baron Cahorn. Am I to abandon my scheme and renounce the treasures that I covet, upon the pretext that the castle which holds them is inaccessible?''

''Evidently not.''

''Should I make an assault upon the castle at the head of a band of adventurers as they did in ancient times?''

''That would be foolish.''

''Can I gain admittance by stealth or cunning?''

''Impossible.''

''Then there is only one way open to me. I must have the owner of the castle invite me to it.''

''That is surely an original method.''

''And how easy! Let us suppose that one day the owner receives a letter warning him that a notorious burglar known as Arsène Lupin is plotting to rob him. What will he do?''

''Send a letter to the Procureur.''

''Who will laugh at him, *because the said Arsène Lupin is actually in prison.* Then, in his anxiety and fear, the simple man will ask the assistance of the first-comer, will he not?''

''Very likely.''

''And if he happens to read in a country

newspaper that a celebrated detective is spending his vacation in a neighboring town——"

"He will seek that detective."

"Of course. But, on the other hand, let us presume that, having foreseen that state of affairs, the said Arsène Lupin has requested one of his friends to visit Caudebec, make the acquaintance of the editor of the *Réveil, a newspaper to which the baron is a subscriber,* and let said editor understand that such person is the celebrated detective—then, what will happen?"

"The editor will announce in the *Réveil* the presence in Caudebec of said detective."

"Exactly; and one of two things will happen: either the fish—I mean Cahorn—will not bite, and nothing will happen; or, what is more likely, he will run and greedily swallow the bait. Thus, behold my Baron Cahorn imploring the assistance of one of my friends against me."

"Original, indeed!"

"Of course, the pseudo-detective at first refuses to give any assistance. On top of that comes the telegram from Arsène Lupin. The frightened baron rushes once more to my friend and offers him a definite sum of money for his services. My friend accepts, summons two members of our band, who, during the night, whilst Cahorn is under the watchful eye of his protector, removes certain articles by way of the window and lowers them with ropes into a nice little launch chartered for the occasion. Simple, isn't it?"

"Marvelous! Marvelous!" exclaimed Ganimard. "The boldness of the scheme and the ingenuity of all its details are beyond criticism. But who is the detective whose name and fame served as a magnet to attract the baron and draw him into your net?"

"There is only one name could do it—only one."

"And that is?"

"Arsène Lupin's personal enemy—the most illustrious Ganimard."

"I?"

"Yourself, Ganimard. And, really, it is very funny. If you go there, and the baron decides to talk, you will find that it will be your duty to arrest yourself, just as you arrested me in America. Hein! the revenge is really amusing: I cause Ganimard to arrest Ganimard."

Arsène Lupin laughed heartily. The detective, greatly vexed, bit his lips; to him

the joke was quite devoid of humor. The
arrival of a prison-guard gave Ganimard an
opportunity to recover himself. The man
brought Arsène Lupin's luncheon, furnished
by a neighboring restaurant. After deposit-
ing the tray upon the table, the guard retired. Lupin broke his bread, ate a few
morsels, and continued:

"But, rest easy, my dear Ganimard, you
will not go to Malaquis. I can tell you something that will astonish you: the Cahorn affair is on the point of being settled."

"Excuse me; I have just seen the Chief of
the Sureté."

"What of that? Does Mon. Dudouis know
my business better than I do myself? You
will learn that Ganimard—excuse me—that
the pseudo-Ganimard still remains on very
good terms with the baron. The latter has
authorized him to negotiate a very delicate
transaction with me, and, at the present moment, in consideration of a certain sum, it is
probable that the baron has recovered possession of his pictures and other treasures.
And on their return, he will withdraw his
complaint. Thus, there is no longer any
theft, and the law must abandon the case."

Ganimard regarded the prisoner with a bewildered air.

"And how do you know all that?"

"I have just received the telegram I was expecting."

"You have just received a telegram?"

"This very moment, my dear friend. Out of politeness, I did not wish to read it in your presence. But if you will permit me——"

"You are joking, Lupin."

"My dear friend, if you will be so kind as to break that egg, you will learn for yourself that I am not joking."

Mechanically, Ganimard obeyed, and cracked the egg-shell with the blade of a knife. He uttered a cry of surprise. The shell contained nothing but a small piece of blue paper. At the request of Arsène he unfolded it. It was a telegram, or rather a portion of a telegram from which the post-marks had been removed. It read as follows:

"Contract closed. Hundred thousand balls delivered. All well."

"One hundred thousand balls?" said Ganimard.

"Yes, one hundred thousand francs. Very little, but then, you know, these are hard times....And I have some heavy bills to

meet. If you only knew my budget....living
in the city comes very high.''

Ganimard arose. His ill humor had disappeared. He reflected for a moment, glancing
over the whole affair in an effort to discover
a weak point; then, in a tone and manner
that betrayed his admiration of the prisoner,
he said:

''Fortunately, we do not have a dozen such
as you to deal with; if we did, we would have
to close up shop.''

Arsène Lupin assumed a modest air, as
he replied:

''Bah! a person must have some diversion
to occupy his leisure hours, especially when
he is in prison.''

''What!'' exclaimed Ganimard, ''your
trial, your defense, the examination—isn't
that sufficient to occupy your mind?''

''No, because I have decided not to be present at my trial.''

''Oh! oh!''

Arsène Lupin repeated, positively:

''I shall not be present at my trial.''

''Really!''

''Ah! my dear monsieur, do you suppose
I am going to rot upon the wet straw? You
insult me. Arsène Lupin remains in prison

just as long as it pleases him, and not one minute more.''

''Perhaps it would have been more prudent if you had avoided getting there,'' said the detective, ironically.

''Ah! monsieur jests? Monsieur must remember that he had the honor to effect my arrest. Know then, my worthy friend, that no one, not even you, could have placed a hand upon me if a much more important event had not occupied my attention at that critical moment.''

''You astonish me.''

''A woman was looking at me, Ganimard, and I loved her. Do you fully understand what that means: to be under the eyes of a woman that one loves? I cared for nothing in the world but that. And that is why I am here.''

''Permit me to say: you have been here a long time.''

''In the first place, I wished to forget. Do not laugh; it was a delightful adventure and it is still a tender memory. Besides, I have been suffering from neurasthenia. Life is so feverish these days that it is necessary to take the 'rest cure' occasionally, and I find

this spot a sovereign remedy for my tired
nerves.''

"Arsène Lupin, you are not a bad fellow,
after all.''

"Thank you,'' said Lupin. "Ganimard,
this is Friday. On Wednesday next, at four
o'clock in the afternoon, I will smoke my
cigar at your house in the rue Pergolese.''

"Arsène Lupin, I will expect you.''

They shook hands like two old friends who
valued each other at their true worth; then
the detective stepped to the door.

"Ganimard!''

"What is it?'' asked Ganimard, as he
turned back.

"You have forgotten your watch.''

"My watch?''

"Yes, it strayed into my pocket.''

He returned the watch, excusing himself:

"Pardon me....a bad habit. Because they
have taken mine is no reason why I should
take yours. Besides, I have a chronometer
here that satisfies me fairly well.''

He took from the drawer a large gold
watch and heavy chain.

"From whose pocket did that come?''
asked Ganimard.

Arsène Lupin gave a hasty glance at the initials engraved on the watch.

"J. B.....Who the devil can that be?.... Ah! yes, I remember. Jules Bouvier, the judge who conducted my examination. A charming fellow!....

CHAPTER III

ARSÈNE LUPIN had just finished his repast and taken from his pocket an excellent cigar, with a gold band, which he was examining with unusual care, when the door of his cell was opened. He had barely time to throw the cigar into the drawer and move away from the table. The guard entered. It was the hour for exercise.

"I was waiting for you, my dear boy," exclaimed Lupin, in his accustomed good humor.

They went out together. As soon as they had disappeared at a turn in the corridor, two men entered the cell and commenced a minute examination of it. One was Inspector Dieuzy; the other was Inspector Folenfant. They wished to verify their suspicion that Arsène Lupin was in communication with his accomplices outside of the prison. On the preceding evening, the *Grand Journal* had published these lines addressed to its court reporter:

"Monsieur:

"In a recent article you referred to me in most unjustifiable terms. Some days before the opening of my trial I will call you to account.   ARSÈNE LUPIN."

The handwriting was certainly that of Arsène Lupin. Consequently, he sent letters; and, no doubt, received letters. It was certain that he was preparing for that escape thus arrogantly announced by him.

The situation had become intolerable. Acting in conjunction with the examining judge, the chief of the Sûreté, Mon. Dudouis, had visited the prison and instructed the gaoler in regard to the precautions necessary to insure Lupin's safety. At the same time, he sent the two men to examine the prisoner's cell. They raised every stone, ransacked the bed, did everything customary in such a case, but they discovered nothing, and were about to abandon their investigation when the guard entered hastily and said:

"The drawer....look in the table-drawer. When I entered just now he was closing it."

They opened the drawer, and Dieuzy exclaimed:

"Ah! we have him this time."

Folenfant stopped him.

"Wait a moment. The chief will want to make an inventory."

"This is a very choice cigar."

"Leave it there, and notify the chief."

Two minutes later Mon. Dudouis examined the contents of the drawer. First he discovered a bundle of newspaper clippings relating to Arsène Lupin taken from the *Argus de la Presse,* then a tobacco-box, a pipe, some paper called "onion-peel," and two books. He read the titles of the books. One was an English edition of Carlyle's "Hero-worship"; the other was a charming elzevir, in modern binding, the "Manual of Epictetus," a German translation published at Leyden in 1634. On examining the books, he found that all the pages were underlined and annotated. Were they prepared as a code for correspondence, or did they simply express the studious character of the reader? Then he examined the tobacco-box and the pipe. Finally, he took up the famous cigar with its gold band.

"Fichtre!" he exclaimed. "Our friend smokes a good cigar. It's a Henry Clay."

With the mechanical action of an habitual smoker, he placed the cigar close to his ear and squeezed it to make it crack. Immedi-

ately he uttered a cry of surprise. The cigar
had yielded under the pressure of his fingers.
He examined it more closely, and quickly de-
tected something white between the leaves of
tobacco. Delicately, with the aid of a pin, he
withdrew a roll of very thin paper, scarcely
larger than a toothpick. It was a letter. He
unrolled it, and found these words, written in
a feminine handwriting:

"The basket has taken the place of the
others. Eight out of ten are ready. On
pressing the outer foot the plate goes down-
ward. From twelve to sixteen every day,
H-P will wait. But where? Reply at once.
Rest easy; your friend is watching over you."

Mon. Dudouis reflected a moment, then
said:

"It is quite clear .... the basket .... the
eight compartments....From twelve to sixteen means from twelve to four o'clock."

"But this H-P, that will wait?"

"H-P must mean automobile. H-P, horse-
power, is the way they indicate the strength
of the motor. A twenty-four H-P is an automobile of twenty-four horsepower."

Then he rose, and asked:

"Had the prisoner finished his breakfast?"

"Yes."

"And as he has not yet read the message, which is proved by the condition of the cigar, it is probable that he has just received it."

"How?"

"In his food. Concealed in his bread or in a potato, perhaps."

"Impossible. His food was allowed to be brought in simply to trap him, but we have never found anything in it."

"We will look for Lupin's reply this evening. Detain him outside for a few minutes. I shall take this to the examining judge, and, if he agrees with me, we will have the letter photographed at once, and in an hour you can replace the letter in the drawer in a cigar similar to this. The prisoner must have no cause for suspicion."

It was not without a certain curiosity that Mon. Dudouis returned to the prison in the evening, accompanied by Inspector Dieuzy. Three empty plates were sitting on the stove in the corner.

"He has eaten?"

"Yes," replied the guard.

"Dieuzy, please cut that macaroni into very small pieces, and open that bread-roll ....Nothing?"

"No, chief."

Mon. Dudouis examined the plates, the fork, the spoon, and the knife—an ordinary knife with a rounded blade. He turned the handle to the left; then to the right. It yielded and unscrewed. The knife was hollow, and served as a hiding-place for a sheet of paper.

"Peuh!" he said, "that is not very clever for a man like Arsène. But we mustn't lose any time. You, Dieuzy, go and search the restaurant."

Then he read the note:

"I trust to you, H-P will follow at a distance every day. I will go ahead. Au revoir, dear friend."

"At last," cried Mon. Dudouis, rubbing his hands, gleefully, "I think we have the affair in our own hands. A little strategy on our part, and the escape will be a success in so far as the arrest of his confederates are concerned."

"But if Arsène Lupin slips through your fingers?" suggested the guard.

"We will have a sufficient number of men to prevent that. If, however, he displays too much cleverness, ma foi, so much the worse for him! As to his band of robbers, since the chief refuses to speak, the others must.

* * * * * *

And, as a matter of fact, Arsène Lupin had very little to say. For several months, Mon. Jules Bouvier, the examining judge, had exerted himself in vain. The investigation had been reduced to a few uninteresting arguments between the judge and the advocate, Maître Danval, one of the leaders of the bar. From time to time, through courtesy, Arsène Lupin would speak. One day he said:

"Yes, monsieur, le judge, I quite agree with you: the robbery of the Crédit Lyonnais, the theft in the rue de Babylone, the issue of the counterfeit bank-notes, the burglaries at the various châteaux, Armesnil, Gouret, Imblevain, Groseillers, Malaquis, all my work, monsieur, I did it all."

"Then will you explain to me——"

"It is useless. I confess everything in a lump, everything and even ten times more that you know nothing about."

Wearied by his fruitless task, the judge had suspended his examinations, but he resumed them after the two intercepted messages were brought to his attention; and regularly, at mid-day, Arsène Lupin was taken from the prison to the Dépôt in the prison-van with a certain number of other

prisoners.   They returned about three or
four o'clock.

Now, one afternoon, this return trip was
made under unusual conditions. The other
prisoners not having been examined, it was
decided to take back Arsène Lupin first, and
thus he found himself alone in the vehicle.

These prison-vans, vulgarly called "pa-
niers à salade"—or salad-baskets—are divided lengthwise by a central corridor from
which open ten compartments, five on either
side. Each compartment is so arranged that
the occupant must assume and retain a sitting posture, and, consequently, the five prisoners are seated one upon the other, and yet
separated one from the other by partitions.
A municipal guard, standing at one end,
watches over the corridor.

Arsène was placed in the third cell on the
right, and the heavy vehicle started. He carefully calculated when they left the quai de
l'Horloge, and when they passed the Palais
de Justice. Then, about the centre of the
bridge Saint Michel, with his outer foot, that
is to say, his right foot, he pressed upon the
metal plate that closed his cell. Immediately
something clicked, and the metal plate moved.

He was able to ascertain that he was located between the two wheels.

He waited, keeping a sharp look-out. The vehicle was proceeding slowly along the boulevard Saint Michel. At the corner of Saint Germain it stopped. A truck horse had fallen. The traffic having been interrupted, a vast throng of fiacres and omnibuses had gathered there. Arsène Lupin looked out. Another prison-van had stopped close to the one he occupied. He moved the plate still farther, put his foot on one of the spokes of the wheel and leaped to the ground. A coachman saw him, roared with laughter, then tried to raise an outcry, but his voice was lost in the noise of the traffic that had commenced to move again. Moreover, Arsène Lupin was already far away.

He had run for a few steps; but, once upon the sidewalk, he turned and looked around; he seemed to scent the wind like a person who is uncertain which direction to take. Then, having decided, he put his hands in his pockets, and, with the careless air of an idle stroller, he proceeded up the boulevard. It was a warm, bright autumn day, and the cafés were full. He took a seat on the terrace of one of them. He ordered a bock and a package of cigarettes. He emptied his glass slowly, smoked one cigarette and lighted a second. Then he asked the waiter to send the proprietor to him. When the proprietor came, Arsène spoke to him in a voice loud enough to be heard by everyone:

"I regret to say, monsieur, I have forgotten my pocketbook. Perhaps, on the strength of my name, you will be pleased to give me credit for a few days. I am Arsène Lupin."

The proprietor looked at him, thinking he was joking. But Arsène repeated:

"Lupin, prisoner at the Santé, but now a fugitive. I venture to assume that the name inspires you with perfect confidence in me."

And he walked away, amidst shouts of laughter, whilst the proprietor stood amazed.

Lupin strolled along the rue Soufflot, and turned into the rue Saint Jacques. He pursued his way slowly, smoking his cigarettes and looking into the shop-windows. At the Boulevard de Port Royal he took his bearings, discovered where he was, and then walked in the direction of the rue de la Santé. The high forbidding walls of the prison were now before him. He pulled his hat forward to shape his face; then, apporaching the sentinel, he asked:

"Is this the prison de la Santé?"

"Yes."

"I wish to regain my cell. The van left me on the way, and I would not abuse——"

"Now, young man, move along—quick!" growled the sentinel.

"Pardon me, but I must pass through that gate. And if you prevent Arsène Lupin from entering the prison it will cost you dear, my friend."

"Arsène Lupin! What are you talking about!"

"I am sorry I haven't a card with me," said Arsène, fumbling in his pockets.

The sentinel eyed him from head to foot, in astonishment. Then, without a word, he rang a bell. The iron gate was partly opened, and Arsène stepped inside. Almost immediately he encountered the keeper of the prison, gesticulating and feigning a violent anger. Arsène smiled and said:

"Come, monsieur, don't play that game with me. What! they take the precaution to carry me alone in the van, prepare a nice little obstruction, and imagine I am going to take to my heels to rejoin my friends. Well, and what about the twenty agents of the Sûreté who accompanied us on foot, in fiacres

and on bicycles? No, the arrangement did
not please me. I should not have got away
alive. Tell me, monsieur, did they count on
that?"

He shrugged his shoulders, and added:

"I beg of you, monsieur, not to worry
about me. When I wish to escape I shall not
require any assistance."

On the second day thereafter, the *Echo de
France,* which had apparently become the official reporter of the exploits of Arsène Lupin, it was said that he was one of its principal shareholders—published a most complete
account of this attempted escape. The exact
wording of the messages exchanged between
the prisoner and his mysterious friend, the
means by which that correspondence was
conducted, the complicity of the police, the
promenade on the Boulevard Saint Michel,
the incident at the café Soufflot, everything
was disclosed. It was known that the search
of the restaurant and its waiters by Inspector
Dieuzy had been fruitless. And the public
also learned an extraordinary thing which
demonstrated the infinite variety of resources
that Lupin possessed: the prison-van, in
which he was being carried, was prepared for
the occasion and substituted by his accom-

plices for one of the six vans which did service at the prison.

The next escape of Arsène Lupin was not
doubted by anyone. He announced it himself, in categorical terms, in a reply to Mon.
Bouvier on the day following his attempted
escape. The judge having made a jest about
the affair, Arsène was annoyed, and, firmly
eyeing the judge, he said, emphatically:

"Listen to me, monsieur! I give you my
word of honor that this attempted flight was
simply preliminary to my general plan of escape."

"I do not understand," said the judge.

"It is not necessary that you should understand."

And when the judge, in the course of that
examination which was reported at length in
the columns of the *Echo de France,* when the
judge sought to resume his investigation, Arsène Lupin exclaimed, with an assumed air
of lassitude:

"Mon Dieu, Mon Dieu, what's the use! All
these questions are of no importance!"

"What! No importance?" cried the judge.

"No; because I shall not be present at the
trial."

"You will not be present?"

"No; I have fully decided on that, and
nothing will change my mind."

Such assurance combined with the inexplicable indiscretions that Arsène committed
every day served to annoy and mystify the
officers of the law. There were secrets known
only to Arsène Lupin; secrets that he alone
could divulge. But for what purpose did he
reveal them? And how?

Arsène Lupin was changed to another cell.
The judge closed his preliminary investigation. No further proceedings were taken in
his case for a period of two months, during
which time Arsène was seen almost constantly
lying on his bed with his face turned toward
the wall. The changing of his cell seemed to
discourage him. He refused to see his advocate. He exchanged only a few necessary
words with his keepers.

During the fortnight preceding his trial,
he resumed his vigorous life. He complained
of want of air. Consequently, early every
morning he was allowed to exercise in the
courtyard, guarded by two men.

Public curiosity had not died out; every
day it expected to be regaled with news of
his escape; and, it is true, he had gained a
considerable amount of public sympathy by

reason of his verve, his gayety, his diversity, his inventive genius and the mystery of his life. Arsène Lupin must escape. It was his inevitable fate. The public expected it, and was surprised that the event had been delayed so long. Every morning the Préfet of Police asked his secretary:

"Well, has he escaped yet?"

"No, Monsieur le Préfet."

"To-morrow, probably."

And, on the day before the trial, a gentleman called at the office of the *Grand Journal*, asked to see the court reporter, threw his card in the reporter's face, and walked rapidly away. These words were written on the card: "Arsène Lupin always keeps his promises."

*   *   *   *   *   *

It was under these conditions that the trial commenced. An enormous crowd gathered at the court. Everybody wished to see the famous Arsène Lupin. They had a gleeful anticipation that the prisoner would play some audacious pranks upon the judge. Advocates and magistrates, reporters and men of the world, actresses and society women were crowded together on the benches provided for the public.

It was a dark, sombre day, with a steady downpour of rain. Only a dim light pervaded the courtroom, and the spectators caught a very indistinct view of the prisoner when the guards brought him in. But his heavy, shambling walk, the manner in which he dropped into his seat, and his passive, stupid appearance were not at all prepossessing. Several times his advocate—one of Mon. Danval's assistants—spoke to him, but he simply shook his head and said nothing.

The clerk read the indictment, then the judge spoke:

"Prisoner at the bar, stand up. Your name, age, and occupation?"

Not receiving any reply, the judge repeated:

"Your name? I ask you your name?"

A thick, slow voice muttered:

"Baudru, Désiré."

A murmur of surprise pervaded the courtroom. But the judge proceeded:

"Baudru, Désiré? Ah! a new alias! Well, as you have already assumed a dozen different names and this one is, no doubt, as imaginary as the others, we will adhere to the name of Arsène Lupin, by which you are more generally known."

The judge referred to his notes, and continued:

"For, despite the most diligent search, your past history remains unknown. Your case is unique in the annals of crime. We know not whom you are, whence you came, your birth and breeding—all is a mystery to us. Three years ago you appeared in our midst as Arsène Lupin, presenting to us a strange combination of intelligence and perversion, immorality and generosity. Our knowledge of your life prior to that date is vague and problematical. It may be that the man called Rostat who, eight years ago, worked with Dickson, the prestidigitator, was none other than Arsène Lupin. It is probable that the Russian student who, six years ago, attended the laboratory of Doctor Altier at the Saint Louis Hospital, and who often astonished the doctor by the ingenuity of his hypotheses on subjects of bacteriology and the boldness of his experiments in diseases of the skin, was none other than Arsène Lupin. It is probable, also, that Arsène Lupin was the professor who introduced the Japanese art of jiu-jitsu to the Parisian public. We have some reason to believe that Arsène Lupin was the bicyclist who won the Grand

Prix de l'Exposition, received his ten thousand francs, and was never heard of again.
Arsène Lupin may have been, also, the person who saved so many lives through the little dormer-window at the Charity Bazaar;
and, at the same time, picked their pockets.''

The judge paused for a moment, then continued:

''Such is that epoch which seems to have
been utilized by you in a thorough prepara-
tion for the warfare you have since waged
against society; a methodical apprenticeship
in which you developed your strength, energy
and skill to the highest point possible. Do
you acknowledge the accuracy of these
facts?''

During this discourse the prisoner had
stood balancing himself, first on one foot,
then on the other, with shoulders stooped and
arms inert. Under the strongest light one
could observe his extreme thinness, his hollow cheeks, his projecting cheek-bones, his
earthen-colored face dotted with small red
spots and framed in a rough, straggling
beard. Prison life had caused him to age
and wither. He had lost the youthful face
and elegant figure that we had seen portrayed
so often in the newspapers.

It appeared as if he had not heard the
question propounded by the judge. Twice it
was repeated to him. Then he raised his
eyes, seemed to reflect, then, making a desperate effort, he murmured:

"Baudru, Désiré."

The judge smiled, as he said:

"I do not understand the theory of your
defense, Arsène Lupin. If you are seeking
to avoid responsibility for your crimes on
the ground of imbecility, such a line of defense is open to you. But I shall proceed with
the trial and pay no heed to your vagaries."

He then narrated at length the various
thefts, swindles and forgeries charged
against Lupin. Sometimes he questioned the
prisoner, but the latter simply grunted or remained silent. The examination of witnesses commenced. Some of the evidence
given was immaterial; other portions of it
seemed more important, but through all of it
there ran a vein of contradictions and inconsistencies. A wearisome obscurity enveloped
the proceedings, until Detective Ganimard
was called as a witness; then interest was revived.

From the beginning the actions of the veteran detective appeared strange and unac-

countable. He was nervous and ill at ease.
Several times he looked at the prisoner, with
obvious doubt and anxiety. Then, with his
hands resting on the rail in front of him, he
recounted the events in which he had participated, including his pursuit of the prisoner
across Europe and his arrival in America.
He was listened to with great avidity, as his
capture of Arsène Lupin was well known to
everyone through the medium of the press.
Toward the close of his testimony, after re-
ferring to his conversations with Arsène
Lupin, he stopped, twice, embarrassed and
undecided. It was apparent that he was possessed of some thought which he feared to
utter. The judge said to him, sympatheti-
cally:

"If you are ill, you may retire for the
present."

"No, no, but——"

He stopped, looked sharply at the prisoner, and said:

"I ask permission to scrutinize the prisoner at closer range. There is some mystery
about him that I must solve."

He approached the accused man, examined
him attentively for several minutes, then re-

turned to the witness-stand, and, in an almost solemn voice, he said:

"I declare, on oath, that the prisoner now before me is not Arsène Lupin."

A profound silence followed that statement. The judge, nonplused for a moment, exclaimed:

"Ah! What do you mean? That is absurd!"

The detective continued:

"At first sight there is a certain resemblance, but if you carefully consider the nose, the mouth, the hair, the color of the skin, you will see that it is not Arsène Lupin. And the eyes! Did he ever have those alcoholic eyes!"

"Come, come, witness! What do you mean? Do you pretend to say that we are trying the wrong man?"

"In my opinion, yes. Arsène Lupin has, in some manner, contrived to put this poor devil in his place, unless this man is a willing accomplice."

This dramatic dénouement caused much laughter and excitement amongst the spectators. The judge adjourned the trial, and sent for Mon. Bouvier, the gaoler, and guards employed in the prison.

When the trial was resumed, Mon. Bouvier

and the gaoler examined the accused and declared that there was only a very slight resemblance between the prisoner and Arsène
Lupin.

"Well, then!" exclaimed the judge, "who
is this man? Where does he come from?
What is he in prison for?"

Two of the prison-guards were called and
both of them declared that the prisoner was
Arsène Lupin. The judge breathed once
more.

But one of the guards then said:

"Yes, yes, I think it is he."

"What!" cried the judge, impatiently,
"you *think* it is he! What do you mean by
that?"

"Well, I saw very little of the prisoner.
He was placed in my charge in the evening
and, for two months, he seldom stirred, but
laid on his bed with his face to the wall."

"What about the time prior to those two
months?"

"Before that he occupied a cell in another
part of the prison. He was not in cell 24."

Here the head gaoler interrupted, and said:

"We changed him to another cell after his
attempted escape."

"But you, monsieur, you have seen him during those two months?"

"I had no occasion to see him. He was always quiet and orderly."

"And this prisoner is not Arsène Lupin?"

"No."

"Then who is he?" demanded the judge.

"I do not know."

"Then we have before us a man who was substituted for Arsène Lupin, two months ago. How do you explain that?"

"I cannot."

In absolute despair, the judge turned to the accused and addressed him in a conciliatory tone:

"Prisoner, can you tell me how, and since when, you became an inmate of the Prison de la Santé?"

The engaging manner of the judge was calculated to disarm the mistrust and awaken the understanding of the accused man. He tried to reply. Finally, under clever and gentle questioning, he succeeded in framing a few phrases from which the following story was gleaned: Two months ago he had been taken to the Dépôt, examined and released. As he was leaving the building, a free man, he was seized by two guards and placed in

the prison-van. Since then he had occupied
cell 24. He was contented there, plenty to
eat, and he slept well—so he did not complain.

All that seemed probable; and, amidst the
mirth and excitement of the spectators, the
judge adjourned the trial until the story
could be investigated and verified.

*   *   *   *   *   *

The following facts were at once established by an examination of the prison-
records: Eight weeks before a man named
Baudru Désiré had slept at the Dépôt. He
was released next day, and left the Dépôt at
two o'clock in the afternoon. On the same
day at two o'clock, having been examined for
the last time, Arsène Lupin left the Dépôt in
a prison-van.

Had the guards made a mistake? Had they
been deceived by the resemblance and carelessly substituted this man for their prisoner?

Another question suggested itself: Had the
substitution been arranged in advance? In
that event Baudru must have been an accomplice and must have caused his own arrest
for the express purpose of taking Lupin's
place. But then, by what miracle had such a

plan, based on a series of improbable chances, been carried to success?

Baudru Désiré was turned over to the anthropological service; they had never seen anything like him. However, they easily traced his past history. He was known at Courbevois, at Asnières and at Levallois. He lived on alms and slept in one of those ragpicker's huts near the barrier des Ternes. He had disappeared from there a year ago.

Had he been enticed away by Arsène Lupin? There was no evidence to that effect. And even if that was so, it did not explain the flight of the prisoner. That still remained a mystery. Amongst twenty theories which sought to explain it, not one was satisfactory. Of the escape itself, there was no doubt; an escape that was incomprehensible, sensational, in which the public, as well as the officers of the law, could detect a carefully-prepared plan, a combination of circumstances marvelously dove-tailed, whereof the dénouement fully justified the confident prediction of Arsène Lupin: "I shall not be present at my trial."

After a month of patient investigation, the problem remained unsolved. The poor devil of a Baudru could not be kept in prison in-

definitely, and to place him on trial would
be ridiculous. There was no charge against
him. Consequently, he was released; but the
chief of the Sûrété resolved to keep him under
surveillance. This idea originated with
Ganimard. From his point of view there was
neither complicity nor chance. Boudru was
an instrument upon which Arsène Lupin had
played with his extraordinary skill. Baudru,
when set at liberty, would lead them to Arsène Lupin or, at least, to some of his accomplices. The two inspectors, Folenfant and
Dieuzy, were assigned to assist Ganimard.

One foggy morning in January the prison
gates opened and Baudru Désiré stepped
forth—a free man. At first he appeared to
be quite embarrassed, and walked like a person who has no precise idea whither he is going. He followed the rue de la Santé and the
rue Saint Jacques. He stopped in front of an
old-clothes shop, removed his jacket and his
vest, sold his vest on which he realized a few
sous; then, replacing his jacket, he proceeded
on his way. He crossed the Seine. At the
Châtelet an omnibus passed him. He wished
to enter it, but there was no place. The con-
troller advised him to secure a number, so he
entered the waiting-room.

Ganimard called his two assistants, and, without removing his eyes from the waiting-room, he said to them:

"Stop a carriage....no, two. That will be better. I will go with one of you, and we will follow him."

The men obeyed. Yet Baudru did not appear. Ganimard entered the waiting-room. It was empty.

"Idiot that I am!" he muttered, "I forgot there was another exit."

There was an interior corridor extending from the waiting-room to the rue Saint Martin. Ganimard rushed through it and arrived just in time to observe Baudru upon the top of the Batignolles-Jardin des Plantes omnibus as it was turning the corner of the rue de Rivoli. He ran and caught the omnibus. But he had lost his two assistants. He must continue the pursuit alone. In his anger he was inclined to seize his man by the collar without ceremony. Was it not with premeditation and by means of an ingenious ruse that his pretended imbecile had separated him from his assistants?

He looked at Baudru. The latter was asleep on the bench, his head rolling from side to side, his mouth half-opened, and an

incredible expression of stupidity on his
blotched face. No, such an adversary was
incapable of deceiving old Ganimard. It was
a stroke of luck—nothing more.

At the Galleries-Lafayette, the man leaped
from the omnibus and took the La Muette
tramway, following the boulevard Hauss-
mann and the avenue Victor Hugo. Baudru
alighted at La Muette station; and, with a
nonchalant air, strolled into the Bois de Bou-
logne.

He wandered through one path after another, and sometimes retraced his steps.
What was he seeking? Had he any definite
object? At the end of an hour, he appeared
to be faint from fatigue, and, noticing a
bench, he sat down. The spot, not far from
Auteuil, on the edge of a pond hidden
amongst the trees, was absolutely deserted.
After the lapse of another half-hour, Ganimard became impatient and resolved to speak
to the man. He approached and took a seat
beside Baudru, lighted a cigarette, traced
some figures in the sand with the end of his
cane, and said:

"It's a pleasant day."

No response. But, suddenly, the man burst
into laughter, a happy, mirthful laugh, spon-

taneous and irresistible. Ganimard felt his hair stand on end in horror and surprise. It was that laugh, that infernal laugh he knew so well!

With a sudden movement, he seized the man by the collar and looked at him with a keen, penetrating gaze; and found that he no longer saw the man Baudru. To be sure, he saw Baudru; but, at the same time, he saw the other, the real man, Lupin. He discovered the intense life in the eyes, he filled up the shrunken features, he perceived the real flesh beneath the flabby skin, the real mouth through the grimaces that deformed it. Those were the eyes and mouth of the other, and especially his keen, alert, mocking expression, so clear and youthful!

"Arsène Lupin, Arsène Lupin," he stammered.

Then, in a sudden fit of rage, he seized Lupin by the throat and tried to hold him down. In spite of his fifty years, he still possessed unusual strength, whilst his adversary was apparently in a weak condition. But the struggle was a brief one. Arsène Lupin made only a slight movement, and, as suddenly as he had made the attack, Ganimard released his hold. His right arm fell inert, useless.

"If you had taken lessons in jiu-jitsu a
the quai des Orfèvres," said Lupin, "yo·
would know that that blow is called udi-shi
ghi in Japanese. A second more, and I woul·
have broken your arm and that would hav·
been just what you deserve. I am surprise·
that you, an old friend whom I respect an·
before whom I voluntarily expose my incog·
nito, should abuse my confidence in that vio·
lent manner. It is unworthy—Ah! What'·
the matter?"

Ganimard did not reply. That escape fo·
which he deemed himself responsible—was i·
not he, Ganimard, who, by his sensational evi·
dence, had led the court into a serious error·
That escape appeared to him like a dar·
cloud on his professional career. A tea·
rolled down his cheek to his gray moustache·

"Oh! mon Dieu, Ganimard, don't take i·
to heart. If you had not spoken, I woul·
have arranged for some one else to do it·
I couldn't allow poor Baudru Désiré to b·
convicted."

"Then," murmured Ganimard, "it wa·
you that was there? And now you are here?'·

"It is I, always I, only I."

"Can it be possible?"

"Oh, it is not the work of a sorcerer. Simply, as the judge remarked at the trial, the apprenticeship of a dozen years that equips a man to cope successfully with all the obstacles in life.''

''But your face? Your eyes?''

''You can understand that if I worked eighteen months with Doctor Altier at the Saint-Louis hospital, it was not out of love for the work. I considered that he, who would one day have the honor of calling himself Arsène Lupin, ought to be exempt from the ordinary laws governing appearance and identity. Appearance? That can be modified at will. For instance, a hypodermic injection of paraffine will puff up the skin at the desired spot. Pyrogallic acid will change your skin to that of an Indian. The juice of the greater celandine will adorn you with the most beautiful eruptions and tumors. Another chemical affects the growth of your beard and hair; another changes the tone of your voice. Add to that two months of dieting in cell 24; exercises repeated a thousand times to enable me to hold my features in a certain grimace, to carry my head at a certain inclination, and adapt my back and shoulders to a stooping posture. Then five

drops of atropine in the eyes to make them
haggard and wild, and the trick is done.''

''I do not understand how you deceived the
guards.''

''The change was progressive. The evolu-
tion was so gradual that they failed to
notice it.''

''But Baudru Désiré?''

''Baudru exists. He is a poor, harmless
fellow whom I met last year; and, really, he
bears a certain resemblance to me. Considering my arrest as a possible event, I took
charge of Baudru and studied the points
wherein we differed in appearance with a
view to correct them in my own person. My
friends caused him to remain at the Dépôt
overnight, and to leave there next day about
the same hour as I did—a coincidence easily
arranged. Of course, it was necessary to have
a record of his detention at the Dépôt in
order to establish the fact that such a person
was a reality; otherwise, the police would
have sought elsewhere to find out my identity.
But, in offering to them this excellent Baudru, it was inevitable, you understand, inevitable that they would seize upon him, and,
despite the insurmountable difficulties of a
substitution, they would prefer to believe in

a substitution rather than confess their ignorance.''

''Yes, yes, of course,'' said Ganimard.

''And then,'' exclaimed Arsène Lupin, ''I held in my hands a trump-card: an anxious public watching and waiting for my escape. And that is the fatal error into which you fell, you and the others, in the course of that fascinating game pending between me and the officers of the law wherein the stake was my liberty. And you supposed that I was playing to the gallery; that I was intoxicated with my success. I, Arsène Lupin, guilty of such weakness! Oh, no! And, no longer ago than the Cahorn affair, you said: When Arsène Lupin cries from the housetops that he will escape, he has some object in view.'' But, sapristi, you must understand that in order to escape I must create, in advance, a public belief in that escape, a belief amounting to an article of faith, an absolute conviction, a reality as glittering as the sun. And I did create that belief that Arsène Lupin would escape, that Arsène Lupin would not be present at his trial. And when you gave your evidence and said: ''That man is not Arsène Lupin,'' everybody was prepared to believe you. Had one person doubted it,

had any one uttered this simple restriction:
Suppose it is Arsène Lupin?—from that moment, I was lost. If anyone had scrutinized
my face, not imbued with the idea that I was
not Arsène Lupin, as you and the others did
at my trial, but with the idea that I might
be Arsène Lupin; then, despite all my precautions, I should have been recognized. But
I had no fear. Logically, psychologically, no
one could entertain the idea that I was Arsène Lupin.''

He grasped Ganimard's hand.

''Come, Ganimard, confess that on the
Wednesday after our conversation in the
prison de la Santé, you expected me at your
house at four o'clock, exactly as I said I
would go.''

''And your prison-van?'' said Ganimard,
evading the question.

''A bluff! Some of my friends secured that
old unused van and wished to make the attempt. But I considered it impracticable
without the concurrence of a number of unusual circumstances. However, I found it
useful to carry out that attempted escape and
give it the widest publicity. An audaciously
planned escape, though not completed, gave

to the succeeding one the character of reality simply by anticipation."

"So that the cigar...."

"Hollowed by myself, as well as the knife."

"And the letters?"   ·

"Written by me."

"And the mysterious correspondent?"

"Did not exist."

Ganimard reflected a moment, then said:

"When the anthropological service had Baudru's case under consideration, why did they not perceive that his measurements coincided with those of Arsène Lupin?"

"My measurements are not in existence."

"Indeed!"

"At least, they are false. I have given considerable attention to that question. In the first place, the Bertillon system records the visible marks of identification—and you have seen that they are not infallible—and, after that, the measurements of the head, the fingers, the ears, etc. Of course, such measurements are more or less infallible."

"Absolutely."

"No; but it costs money to get around them. Before we left America, one of the employees of the service there accepted so much money to insert false figures in my

measurements. Consequently, Baudru's measurements should not agree with those of Arsène Lupin.''

After a short silence, Ganimard asked:

''What are you going to do now?''

''Now,'' replied Lupin, ''I am going to
take a rest, enjoy the best of food and drink
and gradually recover my former healthy
condition. It is all very well to become Baudru or some other person, on occasion, and
to change your personality as you do your
shirt, but you soon grow weary of the
change. I feel exactly as I imagine the man
who lost his shadow must have felt, and I
shall be glad to be Arsène Lupin once more.''

He walked to and fro for a few minutes,
then, stopping in front of Ganimard, he said:

''You have nothing more to say, I suppose?''

''Yes. I should like to know if you intend
to reveal the true state of facts connected
with your escape. The mistake that I
made——''

''Oh! no one will ever know that it was
Arsène Lupin who was discharged. It is to
my own interest to surround myself with
mystery, and therefore I shall permit my
escape to retain its almost miraculous char-

acter. So, have no fear on that score, my dear friend. I shall say nothing. And now, good-bye. I am going out to dinner this evening, and have only sufficient time to dress.''

"I thought you wanted a rest.''

"Ah! there are duties to society that one cannot avoid. To-morrow, I shall rest.''

"Where do you dine to-night?''

"With the British Ambassador!''

CHAPTER IV

THE MYSTERIOUS TRAVELLER

THE evening before, I had sent my automobile to Rouen by the highway. I was to travel to Rouen by rail, on my way to visit some friends that live on the banks of the Seine.

At Paris, a few minutes before the train started, seven gentlemen entered my compartment; five of them were smoking. No matter that the journey was a short one, the thought of traveling with such a company was not agreeable to me, especially as the car was built on the old model, without a corridor. I picked up my overcoat, my newspapers and my time-table, and sought refuge in a neighboring compartment.

It was occupied by a lady, who, at sight of me, made a gesture of annoyance that did not escape my notice, and she leaned toward a gentleman who was standing on the step and was, no doubt, her husband. The gentleman scrutinized me closely, and, apparently, my appearance did not displease him, for he

smiled as he spoke to his wife with the air
of one who reassures a frightened child. She
smiled also, and gave me a friendly glance as
if she now understood that I was one of
those gallant men with whom a woman can
remain shut up for two hours in a little box,
six feet square, and have nothing to fear.

Her husband said to her:

"I have an important appointment, my
dear, and cannot wait any longer. Adieu."

He kissed her affectionately and went
away. His wife threw him a few kisses and
waved her handkerchief. The whistle sounded, and the train started.

At that precise moment, and despite the
protests of the guards, the door was opened,
and a man rushed into our compartment. My
companion, who was standing and arranging
her luggage, uttered a cry of terror and fell
upon the seat. I am not a coward—far from
it—but I confess that such intrusions at the
last minute are always disconcerting. They
have a suspicious, unnatural aspect.

However, the appearance of the new arrival greatly modified the unfavorable impression produced by his precipitant action.
He was correctly and elegantly dressed, wore
a tasteful cravat, correct gloves, and his face

was refined and intelligent. But, where the devil had I seen that face before? Because, beyond all possible doubt, I had seen it. And yet the memory of it was so vague and indistinct that I felt it would be useless to try to recall it at that time.

Then, directing my attention to the lady, I was amazed at the pallor and anxiety I saw in her face. She was looking at her neighbor —they occupied seats on the same side of the compartment—with an expression of intense alarm, and I perceived that one of her trembling hands was slowly gliding toward a little traveling bag that was lying on the seat about twenty inches from her. She finished by seizing it and nervously drawing it to her. Our eyes met, and I read in hers so much anxiety and fear that I could not refrain from speaking to her:

"Are you ill, madame? Shall I open the window?"

Her only reply was a gesture indicating that she was afraid of our companion. I smiled, as her husband had done, shrugged my shoulders, and explained to her, in pantomime, that she had nothing to fear, that I was there, and, besides, the gentleman appeared to be a very harmless individual. At

that moment, he turned toward us, scrutinized both of us from head to foot, then settled down in his corner and paid us no more
attention.

After a short silence, the lady, as if she
had mustered all her energy to perform a
desperate act, said to me, in an almost in-
audible voice:

"Do you know who is on our train?"

"Who?"

"He....he....I assure you...."

"Who is he?"

"Arsène Lupin!"

She had not taken her eyes off our companion, and it was to him rather than to me
that she uttered the syllables of that disquieting name. He drew his hat over his
face. Was that to conceal his agitation or,
simply, to arrange himself for sleep? Then I
said to her:

"Yesterday, through contumacy, Arsène
Lupin was sentenced to twenty years' imprisonment at hard labor. Therefore it is
improbable that he would be so imprudent,
to-day, as to show himself in public. Moreover, the newspapers have announced his appearance in Turkey since his escape from
the Santé."

"But he is on this train at the present moment," the lady proclaimed, with the obvious
intention of being heard by our companion;
"my husband is one of the directors in the
penitentiary service, and it was the station-
master himself who told us that a search was
being made for Arsène Lupin."

"They may have been mistaken——"

"No; he was seen in the waiting-room. He
bought a first-class ticket for Rouen."

"Surely, it would be an easy matter to
find him on the train."

"He has disappeared. The guard at the
waiting-room door did not see him pass, and
it is supposed that he had got into the express
that leaves ten minutes after us."

"In that case, they will be sure to catch
him."

"Unless, at the last moment, he leaped
from that train to come here, into our train
....which is quite probable....which is almost certain."

"If so, he will be arrested just the same;
for the employees and guards would no doubt
observe his passage from one train to the
other, and, when we arrive at Rouen, they
will arrest him there."

"Him—never! He will find some means
of escape."

"In that case, I wish him *bon voyage*."

"But, in the meantime, think what he may
do!"

"What?"

"I don't know. He may do anything."

She was greatly agitated, and, truly, the
situation justified, to some extent, her nervous excitement. I was impelled to say to her:

"Of course, there are many strange coinci-
dences, but you need have no fear. Admitting
that Arsène Lupin is on this train, he will
not commit any indiscretion; he will be only
too happy to escape the peril that already
threatens him."

My words did not reassure her, but she remained silent for a time. I unfolded my
newspapers and read the reports of Arsène
Lupin's trial, but, as they contained nothing
that was new to me, I was not greatly interested. Moreover, I was tired and sleepy. I
felt my eyelids close and my head drop.

"But, monsieur, you are not going to
sleep!"

She seized my newspaper, and looked at
me with indignation.

"Certainly not," I said.

"That would be very imprudent."

"Of course," I assented.

I struggled to keep awake. I looked through the window at the landscape and the fleeting clouds, but in a short time all that became confused and indistinct; the image of the nervous lady and the drowsy gentleman were effaced from my memory, and I was buried in the soothing depths of a profound sleep. The tranquillity of my repose was soon disturbed by disquieting dreams, wherein a creature that had played the part and bore the name of Arsène Lupin held an important place. He appeared to me with his back laden with articles of value; he leaped over walls, and plundered castles. But the outlines of that creature, who was no longer Arsène Lupin, assumed a more definite form. He came toward me, growing larger and larger, leaped into the compartment with incredible agility, and landed squarely on my chest. With a cry of fright and pain, I awoke. The man, the traveller, our companion, with his knee on my breast, held me by the throat.

My sight was very indistinct, for my eyes were suffused with blood. I could see the lady, in a corner of the compartment, con-

vulsed with fright. I tried even not to resist.
Besides, I did not have the strength. My
temples throbbed; I was almost strangled.
One minute more, and I would have breathed
my last. The man must have realized it, for
he relaxed his grip, but did not remove his
hand. Then he took a cord, in which he had
prepared a slip-knot, and tied my wrists together. In an instant, I was bound, gagged
and helpless.

Certainly, he accomplished the trick with
an ease and skill that revealed the hand of a
master; he was, no doubt, a professional
thief. Not a word, not a nervous movement;
only coolness and audacity. And I was there,
lying on the bench, bound like a mummy, I—
Arsène Lupin!

It was anything but a laughing matter, and
yet, despite the gravity of the situation, I
keenly appreciated the humor and irony that
it involved. Arsène Lupin seized and bound
like a novice! robbed as if I were an unso-
phisticated rustic—for, you must understand,
the scoundrel had deprived me of my purse
and wallet! Arsène Lupin, a victim, duped,
vanquished....What an adventure!

The lady did not move. He did not even
notice her. He contented himself with pick-

ing up her traveling-bag that had fallen to
the floor and taking from it the jewels, purse,
and gold and silver trinkets that it contained.
The lady opened her eyes, trembled with fear,
drew the rings from her fingers and handed
them to the man as if she wished to spare
him unnecessary trouble. He took the rings
and looked at her. She swooned.

Then, quite unruffled, he resumed his seat,
lighted a cigarette, and proceeded to examine
the treasure that he had acquired. The examination appeared to give him perfect satisfaction.

But I was not so well satisfied. I do not
speak of the twelve thousand francs of which
I had been unduly deprived: that was only
a temporary loss, because I was certain that
I would recover possession of that money
after a very brief delay, together with the
important papers contained in my wallet:
plans, specifications, addresses, lists of cor-
respondents, and compromising letters. But,
for the moment, a more immediate and more
serious question troubled me: How would
this affair end? What would be the outcome
of this adventure?

As you can imagine, the disturbance created by my passage through the Saint-Lazare

station had not escaped my notice. Going to
visit friends who knew me under the name of
Guillaume Berlat, and amongst whom my resemblance to Arsène Lupin was a subject of
many innocent jests, I could not assume a
disguise, and my presence had been remarked. So, beyond question, the commissary of police at Rouen, notified by telegraph,
and assisted by numerous agents, would be
awaiting the train, would question all suspicious passengers, and proceed to search the
cars.

Of course, I had foreseen all that, but it
had not disturbed me, as I was certain that
the police of Rouen would not be any
shrewder than the police of Paris and that I
could escape recognition; would it not be
sufficient for me to carelessly display my
card as "député," thanks to which I had inspired complete confidence in the gate-keeper
at Saint-Lazare? — But the situation was
greatly changed. I was no longer free. It
was impossible to attempt one of my usual
tricks. In one of the compartments, the commissary of police would find Mon. Arsène
Lupin, bound hand and foot, as docile as a
lamb, packed up, all ready to be dumped into
a prison-van. He would have simply to ac-

cept delivery of the parcel, the same as if it were so much merchandise or a basket of fruit and vegetables. Yet, to avoid that shameful dénouement, what could I do—bound and gagged, as I was? And the train was rushing on toward Rouen, the next and only station.

Another problem was presented, in which I was less interested, but the solution of which aroused my professional curiosity. What were the intentions of my rascally companion? Of course, if I had been alone, he could, on our arrival at Rouen, leave the car slowly and fearlessly. But the lady? As soon as the door of the compartment should be opened, the lady, now so quiet and humble, would scream and call for help. That was the dilemma that perplexed me! Why had he not reduced her to a helpless condition similar to mine? That would have given him ample time to disappear before his double crime was discovered.

He was still smoking, with his eyes fixed upon the window that was now being streaked with drops of rain. Once he turned, picked up my time-table, and consulted it.

The lady had to feign a continued lack of consciousness in order to deceive the enemy.

But fits of coughing, provoked by the smoke,
exposed her true condition. As to me, I was
very uncomfortable, and very tired. And I
meditated; I plotted.

The train was rushing on, joyously, intoxicated with its own speed.

Saint Etienne!....At that moment, the
man arose and took two steps toward us,
which caused the lady to utter a cry of alarm
and fall into a genuine swoon. What was the
man about to do? He lowered the window on
our side. A heavy rain was now falling, and,
by a gesture, the man expressed his annoyance at his not having an umbrella or an overcoat. He glanced at the rack. The lady's
umbrella was there. He took it. He also
took my overcoat and put it on.

We were now crossing the Seine. He
turned up the bottoms of his trousers, then
leaned over and raised the exterior latch of
the door. Was he going to throw himself
upon the track? At that speed, it would have
been instant death. We now entered a tunnel. The man opened the door half-way and
stood on the upper step. What folly! The
darkness, the smoke, the noise, all gave a fantastic appearance to his actions. But suddenly, the train diminished its speed. A mo-

ment later it increased its speed, then slowed up again. Probably, some repairs were being made in that part of the tunnel which obliged the trains to diminish their speed, and the man was aware of the fact. He immediately stepped down to the lower step, closed the door behind him, and leaped to the ground. He was gone.

The lady immediately recovered her wits, and her first act was to lament the loss of her jewels. I gave her an imploring look. She understood, and quickly removed the gag that stifled me. She wished to untie the cords that bound me, but I prevented her.

"No, no, the police must see everything exactly as it stands. I want them to see what the rascal did to us."

"Suppose I pull the alarm-bell?"

"Too late. You should have done that when he made the attack on me."

"But he would have killed me. Ah! monsieur, didn't I tell you that he was on this train. I recognized him from his portrait. And now he has gone off with my jewels."

"Don't worry. The police will catch him."

"Catch Arsène Lupin! Never."

"That depends on you, madame. Listen. When we arrive at Rouen, be at the door and

call. Make a noise. The police and the railway employees will come. Tell what you have
seen: the assault made on me and the flight
of Arsène Lupin. Give a description of him
—soft hat, umbrella — yours — gray overcoat...."

"Yours," said she.

"What! mine? Not at all. It was his. I
didn't have any."

"It seems to me he didn't have one when
he came in."

"Yes, yes.... unless the coat was one that
some one had forgotten and left in the rack.
At all events, he had it when he went away,
and that is the essential point. A gray overcoat—remember!....Ah! I forgot. You must
tell your name, first thing you do. Your husband's official position will stimulate the zeal
of the police."

We arrived at the station. I gave her some
further instructions in a rather imperious
tone:

"Tell them my name—Guillaume Berlat.
If necessary, say that you know me. That
will save time. We must expedite the preliminary investigation. The important thing is
the pursuit of Arsène Lupin. Your jewels,

remember! Let there be no mistake. Guillaume Berlat, a friend of your husband.''

"I understand....Guillaume Berlat.''

She was already calling and gesticulating. As soon as the train stopped, several men entered the compartment. The critical moment had come.

Panting for breath, the lady exclaimed:

"Arsène Lupin....he attacked us.... he stole my jewels....I am Madame Renaud ....my husband is a director in the penitentiary service....Ah! here is my brother, Georges Ardelle, director of the Crédit Rouennais....you must know....

She embraced a young man who had just joined us, and whom the commissary saluted. Then she continued, weeping:

"Yes, Arsène Lupin....while monsieur was sleeping, he seized him by the throat.... Mon. Berlat, a friend of my husband.''

The commissary asked:

"But where is Arsène Lupin?''

"He leaped from the train, when passing through the tunnel.''

"Are you sure that it was he?''

"Am I sure! I recognized him perfectly. Besides, he was seen at the Saint-Lazare station. He wore a soft hat——''

"No, a hard felt, like that," said the commissary, pointing to my hat.

"He had a soft hat, I am sure," repeated
Madame Renaud, "and a gray overcoat."

"Yes, that is right," replied the commissary, "the telegram says he wore a gray
overcoat with a black velvet collar."

"Exactly, a black velvet collar," exclaimed
Madame Renaud, triumphantly.

I breathed freely. Ah! the excellent friend
I had in that little woman.

The police agents had now released me. I
bit my lips until they ran blood. Stooping
over, with my handkerchief over my mouth,
an attitude quite natural in a person who has
remained for a long time in an uncomfortable
position, and whose mouth shows the bloody
marks of the gag, I addressed the commissary, in a weak voice:

"Monsieur, it was Arsène Lupin. There is
no doubt about that. If we make haste, he
can be caught yet. I think I may be of some
service to you."

The railway car, in which the crime occurred, was detached from the train to serve
as a mute witness at the official investigation.
The train continued on its way to Havre.
We were then conducted to the station-mas-

ter's office through a crowd of curious spectators.

Then, I had a sudden access of doubt and discretion. Under some pretext or other, I must gain my automobile, and escape. To remain there was dangerous. Something might happen; for instance, a telegram from Paris, and I would be lost.

Yes, but what about my thief? Abandoned to my own resources, in an unfamiliar country, I could not hope to catch him.

"Bah! I must make the attempt," I said to myself. "It may be a difficult game, but an amusing one, and the stake is well worth the trouble."

And when the commissary asked us to repeat the story of the robbery, I exclaimed:

"Monsieur, really, Arsène Lupin is getting the start of us. My automobile is waiting in the courtyard. If you will be so kind as to use it, we can try...."

The commissary smiled, and replied:

"The idea is a good one; so good, indeed, that it is already being carried out. Two of my men have set out on bicycles. They have been gone for some time."

"Where did they go?"

"To the entrance of the tunnel. There,

they will gather evidence, secure witnesses, and follow on the track of Arsène Lupin."

I could not refrain from shrugging my shoulders, as I replied:

"Your men will not secure any evidence or any witnesses."

"Really!"

"Arsène Lupin will not allow anyone to see him emerge from the tunnel. He will take the first road——"

"To Rouen, where we will arrest him."

"He will not go to Rouen."

"Then he will remain in the vicinity, where his capture will be even more certain."

"He will not remain in the vicinity."

"Oh! oh! And where will he hide?"

I looked at my watch, and said:

"At the present moment, Arsène Lupin is prowling around the station at Darnétal. At ten fifty, that is, in twenty-two minutes from now, he will take the train which goes from Rouen to Amiens."

"Do you think so? How do you know it?"

"Oh! it is quite simple. While we were in the car, Arsène Lupin consulted my railway guide. Why did he do it? Was there, not far from the spot where he disappeared, another line of railway, a station upon that

line, and a train stopping at that station? On
consulting my railway guide, I found such
to be the case.''

"Really, monsieur," said the commissary,
"that is a marvelous deduction. I congratulate you on your skill.''

I was now convinced that I had made a
mistake in displaying so much cleverness.
The commissary regarded me with astonishment, and I thought a slight suspicion entered
his official mind....Oh! scarcely that, for the
photographs distributed broadcast by the police department were too imperfect; they presented an Arsène Lupin so different from
the one he had before him, that he could not
possibly recognize me by it. But, all the
same, he was troubled, confused and ill-at-
ease.

There was a momentary silence. Some
doubt and uncertainty caused it. As for myself, I felt extremely uncomfortable. Was
fortune going to turn against me? Control-
ling myself, I laughed and said:

"Mon Dieu! nothing stimulates the comprehension so much as the loss of a pocketbook and the desire to recover it. And it
seems to me that if you will give me two
of your men, we may be able...."

"Oh! I beg of you, monsieur le commis-
saire," cried Madame Renaud, "listen to
Mon. Berlat."

The intervention of my excellent friend
was decisive. Pronounced by her, the wife of
an influential official, the name of Berlat became really my own, and gave me an identity
that no mere suspicion could affect. The
commissary arose, and said:

"Believe me, Monsieur Berlat, I shall be
delighted to see you succeed. I am as much
interested as you are in the arrest of Arsène
Lupin."

He accompanied me to the automobile, and
introduced two of his men, Honoré Massol
and Gaston Delivet, who were assigned to
assist me. My chauffeur cranked up the car
and I took my place at the wheel. A few seconds later, we left the station. I was saved.

Ah! I must confess that in rolling over the
boulevards that surround the old Norman
city, in my swift thirty-five horse-power Mo-
reau-Lepton, I experienced a deep feeling of
pride, and the motor responded, sympathet-
ically, to my desires. At right and left, the
trees flew past us with startling rapidity, and
I, free, out of danger, had simply to arrange
my little personal affairs with the two honest

representatives of the Rouen police who were sitting behind me. Arsène Lupin was going in search of Arsène Lupin!

Modest guardians of social order—Gaston Delivet and Honoré Massol — how valuable was your assistance! What would I have done without you? Without you, many times, at the cross-roads, I might have taken the wrong route! Without you, Arsène Lupin would have made a mistake, and the other would have escaped!

But the end was not yet. Far from it. I had yet to capture the thief and recover the stolen papers. Under no circumstances must my two acolytes be permitted to see those papers, much less to seize them. That was a point that might give me some difficulty.

We arrived at Darnétal three minutes after the departure of the train. True, I had the consolation of learning that a man wearing a gray overcoat with a black velvet collar had taken the train at that station. He had bought a second-class ticket for Amiens. Certainly, my début as a detective was a promising one.

Delivet said to me:

"The train is express, and the next stop is Montérolier-Buchy in nineteen minutes. If we do not reach there before Arsène Lupin, he can proceed to Amiens, or change for the train going to Clères, and, from that point, reach Dieppe or Paris.''

"How far to Montérolier?''

"Twenty-three kilometres.''

"Twenty-three kilometres in nineteen minutes.... We will be there ahead of him.''

We were off again! Never had my faithful Moreau-Repton responded to my impatience with such ardor and regularity. It participated in my anxiety. It indorsed my determination. It comprehended my animosity against that rascally Arsène Lupin. The knave! The traitor!

"Turn to the right,'' cried Delivet, "then to the left.''

We fairly flew, scarcely touching the ground. The mile-stones looked like little timid beasts that vanished at our approach. Suddenly, at a turn of the road, we saw a vortex of smoke. It was the Northern Express. For a kilometre, it was a struggle, side by side, but an unequal struggle in which the issue was certain. We won the race by twenty lengths.

In three seconds we were on the platform standing before the second-class carriages.

The doors were opened, and some passengers alighted, but not my thief. We made a search through the compartments. No sign of Arsène Lupin.

"Sapristi!" I cried, "he must have recognized me in the automobile as we were racing, side by side, and he leaped from the train."

The head-guard of the train confirmed my theory. He had seen a man tumbling down the embankment about two hundred metres from the station."

"Ah! there he is now! crossing the track."

I started in pursuit of the man, followed by my two acolytes, or rather followed by one of them, for the other, Massol, proved himself to be a runner of exceptional speed and endurance. In a few moments, he had made an appreciable gain upon the fugitive. The man noticed it, leaped over a hedge, scampered across a meadow, and entered a thick grove. When we reached this grove, Massol was waiting for us. He went no farther, for fear of losing us.

"Quite right, my dear friend," I said. "After such a run, our victim must be out of wind. We will catch him now."

I examined the surroundings with the idea

of proceeding alone in the arrest of the fugitive, in order to recover my papers, concerning which the authorities would doubtless ask
many disagreeable questions. Then I returned to my companions, and said:

"It is all quite easy. You, Massol, take
your place at the left; you, Delivet, at the
right. From there, you can observe the entire posterior line of the bush, and he cannot
escape without you seeing him, except by that
ravine, and I shall watch it. If he does not
come out voluntarily, I will enter and drive
him out toward one or the other of you. You
have simply to wait. Ah! I forgot: in case I
need you, a pistol shot."

Massot and Delivet walked away to their
respective posts. As soon as they had disappeared, I entered the grove with the greatest
precaution so as to be neither seen nor heard.
I encountered dense thickets, through which
narrow paths had been cut, but the overhang-
ing boughs compelled me to adopt a stooping
posture. One of these paths led to a clearing
in which I found traces of footsteps upon the
wet grass. I followed them; they led me to
the foot of a mound which was surmounted
by a deserted, dilapidated hovel.

"He must be there," I said to myself. "It is a well-chosen retreat."

I crept cautiously to the side of the building. A slight noise informed me that he was there; and, then, through an opening, I saw him. His back was turned toward me. In two bounds, I was upon him. He tried to fire a revolver that he held in his hand. But he had no time. I threw him to the ground, in such a manner that his arms were beneath him, twisted and helpless, whilst I held him down with my knee on his breast.

"Listen, my boy," I whispered in his ear. "I am Arsène Lupin. You are to deliver over to me, immediately and gracefully, my pocketbook and the lady's jewels, and, in return therefor, I will save you from the police and enroll you amongst my friends. One word: yes or no?"

"Yes," he murmured.

"Very good. Your escape, this morning, was well planned. I congratulate you."

I arose. He fumbled in his pocket, drew out a large knife and tried to strike me with it.

"Imbecile!" I exclaimed.

With one hand, I parried the attack; with

the other, I gave him a sharp blow on the
carotid artery. He fell—stunned!

In my pocketbook, I recovered my papers
and bank-notes. Out of curiosity, I took his.
Upon an envelope, addressed to him, I read
his name: Pierre Onfrey. It startled me.
Pierre Onfrey, the assassin of the rue Lafontaine at Auteuil! Pierre Onfrey, he who had
cut the throats of Madame Delbois and her
two daughters. I leaned over him. Yes,
those were the features which, in the compartment, had evoked in me the memory of
a face I could not then recall.

But time was passing. I placed in an envelope two bank-notes of one hundred francs
each, with a card bearing these words: "Arsène Lupin to his worthy colleagues Honoré
Massol and Gaston Delivet, as a slight token
of his gratitude." I placed it in a prominent
spot in the room, where they would be sure
to find it. Beside it, I placed Madame Renaud's hand-bag. Why could I not return it
to the lady who had befriended me? I must
confess that I had taken from it everything
that possessed any interest or value, leaving
there only a shell comb, a stick of rouge Dorin
for the lips, and an empty purse. But, you

know, business is business. And then, really, her husband is engaged in such a dishonorable vocation!

The man was becoming conscious. What was I to do? I was unable to save him or condemn him. So I took his revolver and fired a shot in the air.

"My two acolytes will come and attend to his case," I said to myself, as I hastened away by the road through the ravine. Twenty minutes later, I was seated in my automobile.

At four o'clock, I telegraphed to my friends at Rouen that an unexpected event would prevent me from making my promised visit. Between ourselves, considering what my friends must now know, my visit is postponed indefinitely. A cruel disillusion for them!

At six o'clock I was in Paris. The evening newspapers informed me that Pierre Onfrey had been captured at last.

Next day,—let us not despise the advantages of judicious advertising,—the *Echo de France* published this sensational item:

"Yesterday, near Buchy, after numerous exciting incidents, Arsène Lupin effected the arrest of Pierre Onfrey. The assassin of the rue Lafontaine had robbed Madame Renaud, wife of the director in the penitentiary

service, in a railway carriage on the Paris-
Havre line. Arsène Lupin restored to Madame Renaud the hand-bag that contained
her jewels, and gave a generous recompense
to the two detectives who had assisted him
in making that dramatic arrest.''

CHAPTER V

THE QUEEN'S NECKLACE

WO or three times each year, on occasions of unusual importance, such as the balls at the Austrian Embassy or the soirées of Lady Billingstone, the Countess de Dreux-Soubise wore upon her white shoulders "The Queen's Necklace."

It was, indeed, the famous necklace, the legendary necklace that Bohmer and Bassenge, court jewelers, had made for Madame Du Barry; the veritable necklace that the Cardinal de Rohan-Soubise intended to give to Marie-Antoinette, Queen of France; and the same that the adventuress Jeanne de Valois, Countess de la Motte, had pulled to pieces one evening in February, 1785, with the aid of her husband and their accomplice, Rétaux de Villette.

To tell the truth, the mounting alone was genuine. Rétaux de Villette had kept it, whilst the Count de la Motte and his wife scattered to the four winds of heaven the beautiful stones so carefully chosen by

Bohmer. Later, he sold the mounting to
Gaston de Dreux-Soubise, nephew and heir of
the Cardinal, who re-purchased the few diamonds that remained in the possession of the
English jeweler, Jefferys; supplemented them
with other stones of the same size but of
much inferior quality, and thus restored the
marvelous necklace to the form in which it
had come from the hands of Bohmer and
Bassenge.

For nearly a century, the house of Dreux-
Soubise had prided itself upon the possession
of this historic jewel. Although adverse circumstances had greatly reduced their fortune, they preferred to curtail their household expenses rather than part with this relic
of royalty. More particularly, the present
count clung to it as a man clings to the home
of his ancestors. As a matter of prudence,
he had rented a safety-deposit box at the
Crédit Lyonnais in which to keep it. He went
for it himself on the afternoon of the day on
which his wife wished to wear it, and he,
himself, carried it back next morning.

On this particular evening, at the reception
given at the Palais de Castille, the Countess
achieved a remarkable success; and King
Christian, in whose honor the fête was given,

commented on her grace and beauty. The thousand facets of the diamond sparkled and shone like flames of fire about her shapely neck and shoulders, and it is safe to say that none but she could have borne the weight of such an ornament with so much ease and grace.

This was a double triumph, and the Count de Dreux was highly elated when they returned to their chamber in the old house of the faubourg Saint-Germain. He was proud of his wife, and quite as proud, perhaps, of the necklace that had conferred added lustre to his noble house for four generations. His wife, also, regarded the necklace with an almost childish vanity, and it was not without regret that she removed it from her shoulders and handed it to her husband who admired it as passionately as if he had never seen it before. Then, having placed it in its case of red leather, stamped with the Cardinal's arms, he passed into an adjoining room which was simply an alcove or cabinet that had been cut off from their chamber, and which could be entered only by means of a door at the foot of their bed. As he had done on previous occasions, he hid it on a high

shelf amongst hat-boxes and piles of linen.
He closed the door, and retired.

Next morning, he arose about nine o'clock,
intending to go to the Crédit Lyonnais before
breakfast. He dressed, drank a cup of coffee,
and went to the stables to give his orders.
The condition of one of the horses worried
him. He caused it to be exercised in his presence. Then he returned to his wife, who had
not yet left the chamber. Her maid was
dressing her hair. When her husband entered, she asked:

"Are you going out?"

"Yes, as far as the bank."

"Of course. That is wise."

He entered the cabinet; but, after a few
seconds, and without any sign of astonishment, he asked:

"Did you take it, my dear?"

"What?....No, I have not taken anything."

"You must have moved it."

"Not at all. I have not even opened that
door."

He appeared at the door, disconcerted, and
stammered, in a scarcely intelligible voice:

"You haven't.... It wasn't you?....
Then...."

She hastened to his assistance, and, together, they made a thorough search, throwing the boxes to the floor and overturning the piles of linen. Then the count said, quite discouraged:

"It is useless to look any more. I put it here, on this shelf."

"You must be mistaken."

"No, no, it was on this shelf — nowhere else."

They lighted a candle, as the room was quite dark, and then carried out all the linen and other articles that the room contained. And, when the room was emptied, they confessed, in despair, that the famous necklace had disappeared. Without losing time in vain lamentations, the countess notified the commissary of police, Mon. Valorbe, who came at once, and, after hearing their story, inquired of the count:

"Are you sure that no one passed through your chamber during the night?"

"Absolutely sure, as I am a very light sleeper. Besides, the chamber door was bolted, and I remember unbolting it this morning when my wife rang for her maid."

"And there is no other entrance to the cabinet?"

"None."

"No window?"

"Yes, but it is closed up."

"I will look at it."

Candles were lighted, and Mon. Valorbe observed at once that the lower half of the window was covered by a large press which was, however, so narrow that it did not touch the casement on either side.

"On what does this window open?"

"A small inner court."

"And you have a floor above this?"

"Two; but, on a level with the servant's floor, there is a close grating over the court. That is why this room is so dark."

When the press was moved, they found that the window was fastened, which would not have been the case if anyone had entered that way.

"Unless," said the count, "they went out through our chamber."

"In that case, you would have found the door unbolted."

The commissary considered the situation for a moment, then asked the countess:

"Did any of your servants know that you wore the necklace last evening?"

"Certainly; I didn't conceal the fact. But

nobody knew that it was hidden in that cabinet.''

''No one?''

''No one....unless....

''Be quite sure, madam, as it is a very important point.''

She turned to her husband, and said:

''I was thinking of Henriette.''

''Henriette? She didn't know where we kept it.''

''Are you sure?''

''Who is this woman Henriette?'' asked Mon. Valorbe.

''A school-mate, who was disowned by her family for marrying beneath her. After her husband's death, I furnished an apartment in this house for her and her son. She is clever with her needle and has done some work for me.''

''What floor is she on?''

''Same as ours....at the end of the cordidor....and I think....the window of her kitchen....

''Opens on this little court, does it not?''

''Yes, just opposite ours.''

Mon. Valorbe then asked to see Henriette. They went to her apartment; she was sewing, whilst her son Raoul, about six years old, was sitting beside her, reading. The commissary was surprised to see the wretched apartment that had been provided for the woman. It consisted of one room without a fireplace, and a very small room that served as a kitchen. The commissary proceeded to question her. She appeared to be overwhelmed on learning of the theft. Last evening she had herself dressed the countess and placed the necklace upon her shoulders.

"Good God!" she exclaimed, "it can't be possible!"

"And you have no idea? Not the least suspicion? Is it possible that the thief may have passed through your room?"

She laughed heartily, never supposing that she could be an object of suspicion.

"But I have not left my room. I never go out. And, perhaps, you have not seen?"

She opened the kitchen window, and said:

"See, it is at least three metres to the ledge of the opposite window."

"Who told you that we supposed the theft might have been committed in that way?"

"But....the necklace was in the cabinet, wasn't it?"

"How do you know that?"

"Why, I have always known that it was

kept there at night. It has been mentioned
in my presence.''

Her face, though still young, bore unmis-
takable traces of sorrow and resignation.
And it now assumed an expression of anxiety
as if some danger threatened her. She drew
her son toward her. The child took her hand,
and kissed it affectionately.

When they were alone again, the count said
to the commissary:

''I do not suppose you suspect Henriette.
I can answer for her. She is honesty itself.''

''I quite agree with you,'' replied Mon. Valorbe. ''At most, I thought there might have
been an unconscious complicity. But I confess that even that theory must be abandoned,
as it does not help to solve the problem now
before us.''

The commissary of police abandoned the
investigation, which was now taken up and
completed by the examining judge. He questioned the servants, examined the condition
of the bolt, experimented with the opening
and closing of the cabinet window, and ex-
plored the little court from top to bottom.
All was in vain. The bolt was intact. The
window could not be opened or closed from
the outside.

The inquiries especially concerned Henriette, for, in spite of everything, they always turned in her direction. They made a thorough investigation of her past life, and ascertained that, during the last three years, she had left the house only four times, and her business, on those occasions, was satisfactorily explained. As a matter of fact, she acted as chambermaid and seamstress to the countess, who treated her with great strictness and even severity.

At the end of a week, the examining judge had secured no more definite information than the commissary of police. The judge said:

"Admitting that we know the guilty party, which we do not, we are confronted by the fact that we do not know how the theft was committed. We are brought face to face with two obstacles: a door and a window—both closed and fastened. It is thus a double mystery. How could anyone enter, and, moreover, how could anyone escape, leaving behind him a bolted door and a fastened window?"

At the end of four months, the secret opinion of the judge was that the count and countess, being hard pressed for money, which was their normal condition, had sold the Queen's Necklace. He closed the investigation.

The loss of the famous jewel was a severe blow to the Dreux-Soubise. Their credit being no longer propped up by the reserve fund that such a treasure constituted, they found themselves confronted by more exacting creditors and money-lenders. They were obliged to cut down to the quick, to sell or mortgage every article that possessed any commercial value. In brief, it would have been their ruin, if two large legacies from some distant relatives had not saved them.

Their pride also suffered a downfall, as if they had lost a quartering from their escutcheon. And, strange to relate, it was upon her former schoolmate, Henriette, that the countess vented her spleen. Toward her, the countess displayed the most spiteful feelings, and even openly accused her. First, Henriette was relegated to the servants' quarters, and, next day, discharged.

For some time, the count and countess passed an uneventful life. They traveled a great deal. Only one incident worthy of record occurred during that period. Some months after the departure of Henriette, the countess was surprised when she received and read the following letter, signed by Henriette:

"Madame,

"I do not know how to thank you; for it was you, was it not, who sent me that? It could not be anyone else. No one but you knows where I live. If I am wrong, excuse me, and accept my sincere thanks for your past favors...."

What did the letter mean? The present or past favors of the countess consisted principally of injustice and neglect. Why, then, this letter of thanks?

When asked for an explanation, Henriette replied that she had received a letter, through the mails, enclosing two bank-notes of one thousand francs each. The envelope, which she enclosed with her reply, bore the Paris post-mark, and was addressed in a handwriting that was obviously disguised. Now, whence came those two thousand francs? Who had sent them? And why had they sent them?

Henriette received a similar letter and a like sum of money twelve months later. And a third time; and a fourth; and each year for a period of six years, with this difference, that in the fifth and sixth years the

sum was doubled. There was another difference: the post-office authorities having
seized one of the letters under the pretext
that it was not registered, the last two letters were duly sent according to the postal
regulations, the first dated from Saint-Germain, the other from Suresnes. The writer
signed the first one, "Anquety"; the other,
"Péchard." The addresses that he gave
were false.

At the end of six years, Henriette died,
and the mystery remained unsolved.

*   *   *   *   *   *

All these events are known to the public.
The case was one of those which excite public
interest, and it was a strange coincidence
that this necklace, which had caused such a
great commotion in France at the close of
the eighteenth century, should create a similar commotion a century later. But what
I am about to relate is known only to the
parties directly interested and a few others
from whom the count exacted a promise of
secrecy. As it is probable that some day
or other that promise will be broken, I have
no hesitation in rending the veil and thus
disclosing the key to the mystery, the explanation of the letter published in the morning

papers two days ago; an extraordinary letter which increased, if possible, the mists
and shadows that envelope this inscrutable
drama.

Five days ago, a number of guests were
dining with the Count de Dreux-Soubise.
There were several ladies present, including
his two nieces and his cousin, and the following gentlemen: the president of Essa-
ville, the deputy Bochas, the chevalier Floriani, whom the count had known in Sicily,
and General Marquis de Rouzières, an old
club friend.

After the repast, coffee was served by the
ladies, who gave the gentlemen permission
to smoke their cigarettes, provided they
would not desert the salon. The conversation was general, and finally one of the
guests chanced to speak of celebrated crimes.
And that gave the Marquis de Rouzières,
who delighted to tease the count, an opportunity to mention the affair of the Queen's
Necklace, a subject that the count detested.

Each one expressed his own opinion of
the affair; and, of course, their various theories were not only contradictory but impossible.

"And you, monsieur," said the countess

to the chevalier Floriani, "what is your opinion?"

"Oh! I—I have no opinion, madame."

All the guests protested; for the chevalier had just related in an entertaining manner various adventures in which he had participated with his father, a magistrate at Palermo, and which established his judgment and taste in such matters.

"I confess," said he, "I have sometimes succeeded in unraveling mysteries that the cleverest detectives have renounced; yet I do not claim to be a Sherlock Holmes. Moreover, I know very little about the affair of the Queen's Necklace."

Everybody now turned to the count, who was thus obliged, quite unwillingly, to narrate all the circumstances connected with the theft. The chevalier listened, reflected, asked a few questions, and said:

"It is very strange....at first sight, the problem appears to be a very simple one."

The count shrugged his shoulders. The others drew closer to the chevalier, who continued, in a dogmatic tone:

"As a general rule, in order to find the author of a crime or a theft, it is necessary to determine how that crime or theft was

committed, or, at least, how it could have
been committed. In the present case, nothing
is more simple, because we are face to face,
not with several theories, but with one positive fact, that is to say: the thief could enter
only by the chamber door or the window of
the cabinet. Now, a person cannot open a
bolted door from the outside. Therefore, he
must have entered through the window."

"But it was closed and fastened, and we
found it fastened afterward," declared the
count.

"In order to do that," continued Floriani,
without heeding the interruption, "he had
simply to construct a bridge, a plank or a
ladder, between the balcony of the kitchen
and the ledge of the window, and as the
jewel-case—"

"But I repeat that the window was fastened," exclaimed the count, impatiently.

This time, Floriani was obliged to reply.
He did so with the greatest tranquility, as
if the objection was the most insignificant
affair in the world.

"I will admit that it was; but is there not
a transom in the upper part of the window?"

"How do you know that?"

"In the first place, that was customary in

houses of that date; and, in the second place, without such a transom, the theft cannot be explained.''

''Yes, there is one, but it was closed, the same as the window. Consequently, we did not pay any attention to it.''

''That was a mistake; for, if you had examined it, you would have found that it had been opened.''

''But how?''

''I presume that, like all others, it opens by means of a wire with a ring at the lower end.''

''Yes.''

''And that ring was hanging between the window and the press.''

''Yes, but I do not see—''

''Now, through a hole in the window, a person could, by the aid of some instrument, let us say a poker with a hook at the end, grip the ring, pull down, and open the transom.''

The count laughed, and said:

''Excellent! excellent! Your scheme is very cleverly constructed, but you overlook one thing, monsieur, there is no hole in the window.''

''There was a hole.''

"Nonsense we would have seen it."

"In order to see it, you must look for it,
and no one has looked. The hole is there;
it must be there, at the side of the window,
in the putty. In a vertical direction, of
course."

The count arose. He was greatly excited.
He paced up and down the room, two or
three times, in a nervous manner; then,
approaching Floriani, said:

"Nobody has been in that room since;
nothing has been changed."

"Very well, monsieur, you can easily
satisfy yourself that my explanation is
correct."

"It does not agree with the facts established by the examining judge. You have
seen nothing, you know nothing, and yet you
contradict all that we have seen and all that
we know."

Floriani paid no attention to the count's
petulance. He simply smiled and said:

"Mon Dieu, monsieur, I submit my theory;
that is all. If I am mistaken, you can easily
prove it."

"I will do so at once.... I confess that
your assurance—"

The count muttered a few more words;

then suddenly rushed to the door and passed out. Not a word was uttered in his absence; and this profound silence gave the situation an air of almost tragic importance. Finally, the count returned. He was pale and nervous. He said to his friends, in a trembling voice:

"I beg your pardon....the revelations of the chevalier were so unexpected....I should never have thought...."

His wife questioned him, eagerly:

"Speak....what is it?"

He stammered: "The hole is there, at the very spot, at the side of the window—"

He seized the chevalier's arm, and said to him in am imperious tone:

"Now, monsieur, proceed. I admit that you are right so far, but now....that is not all....go on....tell us the rest of it."

Floriani disengaged his arm gently, and, after a moment, continued:

"Well, in my opinion, this is what happened. The thief, knowing that the countess was going to wear the necklace that evening, had prepared his gangway or bridge during your absence. He watched you through the window and saw you hide the necklace.

Afterward, he cut the glass and pulled the ring.''

"Ah! but the distance was so great that it would be impossible for him to reach the window-fastening through the transom.''

"Well, then, if he could not open the window by reaching through the transom, he must have crawled through the transom.''

"Impossible; it is too small. No man could crawl through it.''

"Then it was not a man,'' declared Floriani.

"What!''

"If the transom is too small to admit a man, it must have been a child.''

"A child!''

"Did you not say that your friend Henriette had a son?''

"Yes; a son named Raoul.''

"Then, in all probability, it was Raoul who committed the theft.''

"What proof have you of that?''

"What proof! Plenty of it.... For instance—''

He stopped, and reflected for a moment, then continued:

"For instance, that gangway or bridge. It is improbable that the child could have brought it from outside the house and carried it away again without being observed. He must have used something close at hand. In the little room used by Henriette as a kitchen, were there not some shelves against the wall on which she placed her pans and dishes?''

''Two shelves, to the best of my memory.''

''Are you sure that those shelves are really fastened to the wooden brackets that support them? For, if they are not, we would be justified in presuming that the child removed them, fastened them together, and thus formed his bridge. Perhaps, also, since there was a stove, we might find the bent poker that he used to open the transom.''

Without saying a word, the count left the room; and, this time, those present did not feel the nervous anxiety they had experienced the first time. They were confident that Floriani was right, and no one was surprised when the count returned and declared:

''It was the child. Everything proves it.''

''You have seen the shelves and the poker?''

''Yes. The shelves have been unnailed, and the poker is there yet.''

But the countess exclaimed:

"You had better say it was his mother. Henriette is the guilty party. She must have compelled her son—"

"No," declared the chevalier, "the mother had nothing to do with it."

"Nonsense! they occupied the same room. The child could not have done it without the mother's knowledge."

"True, they lived in the same room, but all this happened in the adjoining room, during the night, while the mother was asleep."

"And the necklace?" said the count. "It would have been found amongst the child's things."

"Pardon me! He had been out. That morning, on which you found him reading, he had just come from school, and perhaps the commissary of police, instead of wasting his time on the innocent mother, would have been better employed in searching the child's desk amongst his school-books."

"But how do you explain those two thousand francs that Henriette received each year? Are they not evidence of her complicity?"

"If she had been an accomplice, would

she have thanked you for that money? And then, was she not closely watched? But the child, being free, could easily go to a neighboring city, negotiate with some dealer and sell him one diamond or two diamonds, as he might wish, upon condition that the money should be sent from Paris, and that proceeding could be repeated from year to year."

An indescribable anxiety oppressed the Dreux-Soubise and their guests. There was something in the tone and attitude of Floriani—something more that the chevalier's assurance which, from the beginning, had so annoyed the count. There was a touch of irony, that seemed rather hostile than sympathetic. But the count affected to laugh, as he said:

"All that is very ingenious and interesting, and I congratulate you upon your vivid imagination."

"No, not at all," replied Floriani, with the utmost gravity, "I imagine nothing. I simply describe the events as they must have occurred."

"But what do you know about them?"

"What you yourself have told me. I picture to myself the life of the mother and

child down there in the country; the illness
of the mother, the schemes and inventions of
the child to sell the precious stones in order
to save his mother's life, or, at least, soothe
her dying moments. Her illness overcomes
her. She dies. Years roll on. The child becomes a man; and then—and now I will give
my imagination a free rein—let us suppose
that the man feels a desire to return to the
home of his childhood, that he does so, and
that he meets there certain people who suspect and accuse his mother....do you realize
the sorrow and anguish of such an interview
in the very house wherein the original drama
was played?"

His words seemed to echo for a few seconds
in the ensuing silence, and one could read
upon the faces of the Count and Countess de
Dreux a bewildered effort to comprehend his
meaning and, at the same time, the fear and
anguish of such a comprehension. The count
spoke at last, and said:

"Who are you, monsieur?"

"I? The chevalier Floriani, whom you met
at Palermo, and whom you have been gra-
cious enough to invite to your house on several occasions."

"Then what does this story mean?"

"Oh! nothing at all! It is simply a pas-
time, so far as I am concerned. I endeavor
to depict the pleasure that Henriette's son, if
he still lives, would have in telling you that
he was the guilty party, and that he did it
because his mother was unhappy, as she was
on the point of losing the place of a.....
servant, by which she lived, and because the
child suffered at sight of his mother's sorrow."

He spoke with suppressed emotion, rose
partially and inclined toward the countess.
There could be no doubt that the chevalier
Floriani was Henriette's son. His attitude
and words proclaimed it. Besides, was it
not his obvious intention and desire to be
recognized as such?

The count hesitated. What action would
he take against the audacious guest? Ring?
Provoke a scandal? Unmask the man who
had once robbed him? But that was a long
time ago! And who would believe that absurd story about the guilty child? No; better far to accept the situation, and pretend
not to comprehend the true meaning of it.
So the count, turning to Floriani, exclaimed:

"Your story is very curious, very entertaining; I enjoyed it very much. But what

do you think has become of this young man,
this model son? I hope he has not abandoned
the career in which he made such a brilliant
début.''

''Oh! certainly not.''

''After such a début! To steal the Queen's
Necklace at six years of age; the celebrated
necklace that was coveted by Marie-Antoinette!''

''And to steal it,'' remarked Floriani, falling in with the count's mood, ''without cost-
ing him the slightest trouble, without anyone
thinking to examine the condition of the window, or to observe that the window-sill was
too clean — that window-sill which he had
wiped in order to efface the marks he had
made in the thick dust. We must admit that
it was sufficient to turn the head of a boy of
that age. It was all so easy. He had simply
to desire the thing, and reach out his hand
to get it.''

''And he reached out his hand.''

''Both hands,'' replied the chevalier,
laughing.

His companions received a shock. What
mystery surrounded the life of the so-called
Floriani? How wonderful must have been
the life of that adventurer, a thief at six

years of age, and who, to-day, in search of
excitement or, at most, to gratify a feeling
of resentment, had come to brave his victim
in her own house, audaciously, foolishly, and
yet with all the grace and delicacy of a cour-
teous guest!

He arose and approached the countess to
bid her adieu. She recoiled, unconsciously.
He smiled.

"Oh! Madame, you are afraid of me! Did
I pursue my rôle of parlor-magician a step
too far?"

She controlled herself, and replied, with
her accustomed ease:

"Not at all, monsieur. The legend of that
dutiful son interested me very much, and I
am pleased to know that my necklace had
such a brilliant destiny. But do you not
think that the son of that woman, that Henriette, was the victim of hereditary influence
in the choice of his vocation?"

He shuddered, feeling the point, and replied:

"I am sure of it; and, moreover, his natural tendency to crime must have been very
strong or he would have been discouraged."

"Why so?"

"Because, as you must know, the majority

of the diamonds were false. The only genuine stones were the few purchased from the English jeweler, the others having been sold, one by one, to meet the cruel necessities of life.''

''It was still the Queen's Necklace, monsieur,'' replied the countess, haughtily, ''and that is something that he, Henriette's son, could not appreciate.''

''He was able to appreciate, madame, that, whether true or false, the necklace was nothing more than an object of parade, an emblem of senseless pride.''

The count made a threatening gesture, but his wife stopped him.

''Monsieur,'' she said, ''if the man to whom you allude has the slightest sense of honor—''

She stopped, intimidated by Floriani's cool manner.

''If that man has the slightest sense of honor,'' he repeated.

She felt that she would not gain anything by speaking to him in that manner, and in spite of herself and in spite of her anger and indignation, trembling as she was from humiliated pride, she said to him, almost politely:

"Monsieur, the legend says that Rétaux de Villette, when in possession of the Queen's Necklace, did not disfigure the mounting. He understood that the diamonds were simply the ornament, the accessory, and that the mounting was the essential work, the creation of the artist, and he respected it accordingly. Do you think that this man had the same feeling?"

"I have no doubt that the mounting still exists. The child respected it."

"Well, monsieur, if you should happen to meet him, will you tell him that he unjustly keeps possession of a relic that is the property and pride of a certain family, and that, although the stones have been removed, the Queen's necklace still belongs to the house of Dreux-Soubise. It belongs to us as much as our name or our honor."

The chevalier replied, simply:

"I shall tell him, madame."

He bowed to her, saluted the count and the other guests, and departed.

*   *   *   *   *

Four days later, the countess de Dreux found upon the table in her chamber a red leather case bearing the cardinal's arms. She opened it, and found the Queen's Necklace.

But as all things must, in the life of a man who strives for unity and logic, converge toward the same goal—and as a little advertising never does any harm—on the following day, the *Echo de France* published these sensational lines:

"The Queen's Necklace, the famous historical jewelry stolen from the family of Dreux-Soubise, has been recovered by Arsène Lupin, who hastened to restore it to its rightful owner. We cannot too highly commend such a delicate and chivalrous act."

Chapter VI

 AM frequently asked this question: "How did you make the acquaintance of Arsène Lupin?"

My connection with Arsène Lupin was well known. The details that I gather concerning that mysterious man, the irrefutable facts that I present, the new evidence that I produce, the interpretation that I place on certain acts of which the public has seen only the exterior manifestations without being able to discover the secret reasons or the invisible mechanism, all establish, if not an intimacy, at least amical relations and regular confidences.

But how did I make his acquaintance? Why was I selected to be his historiographer? Why I, and not some one else?

The answer is simple: chance alone presided over my choice; my merit was not considered. It was chance that put me in his way. It was by chance that I was participant in one of his strangest and most mysterious

adventures; and by chance that I was an
actor in a drama of which he was the marvelous stage director; an obscure and intri-
cate drama, bristling with such thrilling
events that I feel a certain embarrassment in
undertaking to describe it.

The first act takes place during that
memorable night of 22 June, of which so
much has already been said. And, for my
part, I attribute the anomalous conduct of
which I was guilty on that occasion to the unusual frame of mind in which I found myself
on my return home. I had dined with some
friends at the Cascade restaurant, and, the
entire evening, whilst we smoked and the or-
chestra played melancholy waltzes, we talked
only of crimes and thefts, and dark and
frightful intrigues. That is always a poor
overture to a night's sleep.

The Saint-Martins went away in an automobile. Jean Daspry—that delightful, heed-
less Daspry who, six months later, was killed
in such a tragic manner on the frontier of
Morocco—Jean Daspry and I returned on
foot through the dark, warm night. When
we arrived in front of the little house in
which I had lived for a year at Neuilly, on the
boulevard Maillot, he said to me:

"Are you never afraid?"

"What an idea!"

"But this house is so isolated . . . no neighbors . . . . vacant lots . . . . Really, I am not a coward, and yet——"

"Well, you are very cheering, I must say."

"Oh! I say that as I would say anything else. The Saint-Martins have impressed me with their stories of brigands and thieves."

We shook hands and said good-night. I took out my key and opened the door.

"Well, that is good," I murmured, "Antoine has forgotten to light a candle."

Then I recalled the fact that Antoine was away; I had given him a short leave of absence. Forthwith, I was disagreeably oppressed by the darkness and silence of the night. I ascended the stairs on tiptoe, and reached my room as quickly as possible; then, contrary to my usual habit, I turned the key and pushed the bolt.

The light of my candle restored my courage. Yet I was careful to take my revolver from its case—a large, powerful weapon— and place it beside my bed. That precaution completed my reassurance. I laid down and, as usual, took a book from my night-table to read myself to sleep. Then I received a great surprise. Instead of the paper-knife with which I had marked my place on the preceding evening, I found an envelope, closed with five seals of red wax. I seized it eagerly. It was addressed to me, and marked: "Urgent."

A letter! A letter addressed to me! Who could have put it in that place? Nervously, I tore open the envelope, and read:

"From the moment you open this letter, whatever happens, whatever you may hear, do not move, do not utter one cry. Otherwise you are doomed."

I am not a coward, and, quite as well as another, I can face real danger, or smile at the visionary perils of the imagination. But, let me repeat, I was in an anomalous condition of mind, with my nerves set on edge by the events of the evening. Besides, was there not, in my present situation, something startling and mysterious, calculated to disturb the most courageous spirit?

My feverish fingers clutched the sheet of paper, and I read and re-read those threatening words: "Do not move, do not utter one cry. Otherwise, you are doomed."

"Nonsense!" I thought. "It is a joke; the work of some cheerful idiot."

I was about to laugh—a good loud laugh.
Who prevented me? What haunting fear
compressed my throat?

At least, I would blow out the candle. No,
I could not do it. "Do not move, or you are
doomed," were the words he had written.

These auto-suggestions are frequently
more imperious than the most positive reali-
ties; but why should I struggle against them?
I had simply to close my eyes. I did so.

At that moment, I heard a slight noise, followed by crackling sounds, proceeding from
a large room used by me as a library. A
small room or antechamber was situated between the library and my bedchamber.

The approach of an actual danger greatly
excited me, and I felt a desire to get up, seize
my revolver, and rush into the library. I did
not rise; I saw one of the curtains of the left
window move. There was no doubt about it:
the curtain had moved. It was still moving.
And I saw—oh! I saw quite distinctly—in the
narrow space between the curtains and the
window, a human form; a bulky mass that
prevented the curtains from hanging
straight. And it is equally certain that the
man saw me through the large meshes of the
curtain. Then, I understood the situation.

His mission was to guard me while the others carried away their booty. Should I rise and seize my revolver? Impossible! He was there! At the least movement, at the least cry, I was doomed.

Then came a terrific noise that shook the house; this was followed by lighter sounds, two or three together, like those of a hammer that rebounded. At least, that was the impression formed in my confused brain. These were mingled with other sounds, thus creating a veritable uproar which proved that the intruders were not only bold, but felt themselves secure from interruption.

They were right. I did not move. Was it cowardice? No, rather weakness, a total inability to move any portion of my body, combined with discretion; for why should I struggle? Behind that man, there were ten others who would come to his assistance. Should I risk my life to save a few tapestries and bibelots?

Throughout the night, my torture endured. Insufferable torture, terrible anguish! The noises had stopped, but I was in constant fear of their renewal. And the man! The man who was guarding me, weapon in hand. My fearful eyes remained cast in his direction. And my heart beat! And a profuse perspiration oozed from every pore of my body!

Suddenly, I experienced an immense relief; a milk-wagon, whose sound was familiar to me, passed along the boulevard; and, at the same time, I had an impression that the light of a new day was trying to steal through the closed window-blinds.

At last, daylight penetrated the room; other vehicles passed along the boulevard; and all the phantoms of the night vanished. Then I put one arm out of the bed, slowly and cautiously. My eyes were fixed upon the curtain, locating the exact spot at which I must fire; I made an exact calculation of the movements I must make; then, quickly, I seized my revolver and fired.

I leaped from my bed with a cry of deliverance, and rushed to the window. The bullet had passed through the curtain and the window-glass, but it had not touched the man— for the very good reason that there was none there. Nobody! Thus, during the entire night, I had been hypnotized by a fold of the curtain. And, during that time, the malefactors. . . . Furiously, with an enthusiasm that nothing could have stopped, I turned the key, opened the door, crossed the antechamber, opened another door, and rushed into the library. But amazement stopped me on the threshold, panting, astounded, more astonished than I had been by the absence of the man. All the things that I supposed had been stolen, furniture, books, pictures, old tapestries, everything was in its proper place.

It was incredible. I could not believe my eyes. Notwithstanding that uproar, those noises of removal . . . . I made a tour, I inspected the walls, I made a mental inventory of all the familiar objects. Nothing was missing. And, what was more disconcerting, there was no clue to the intruders, not a sign, not a chair disturbed, not the trace of a footstep.

"Well! Well!" I said to myself, pressing my hands on my bewildered head, "surely I am not crazy! I heard something!"

Inch by inch, I made a careful examination of the room. It was in vain. Unless I could consider this as a discovery: Under a small Persian rug, I found a card—an ordinary playing-card. It was the seven of hearts; it was like any other seven of hearts in French playing-cards, with this slight but curious exception: The extreme point of each of the

seven red spots or hearts was pierced by a
hole, round and regular as if made with the
point of an awl.

Nothing more. A card and a letter found
in a book. But was not that sufficient to affirm that I had not been the plaything of a
dream?

*   *   *   *   *

Throughout the day, I continued my
searches in the library. It was a large room,
much too large for the requirements of such
a house, and the decoration of which attested
the bizarre taste of its founder. The floor
was a mosaic of multicolored stones, formed
into large symmetrical designs. The walls
were covered with a similar mosaic, arranged
in panels, Pompeiian allegories, Byzantine
compositions, frescoes of the Middle Ages.
A Bacchus bestriding a cask. An emperor
wearing a gold crown, a flowing beard, and
holding a sword in his right hand.

Quite high, after the style of an artist's
studio, there was a large window—the only
one in the room. That window being always
open at night, it was probable that the men
had entered through it, by the aid of a ladder.
But, again, there was no evidence. The bottom of the ladder would have left some marks

in the soft earth beneath the window; but
there were none. Nor were there any traces
of footsteps in any part of the yard.

I had no idea of informing the police, because the facts that I had before me were so
absurd and inconsistent. They would laugh
at me. However, as I was then a reporter on
the staff of the *Gil Blas,* I wrote a lengthy account of my adventure and it was published
in that paper on the second day thereafter.
The article attracted some attention, but no
one took it seriously. They regarded it as a
work of fiction rather than a story of real
life. The Saint-Martins rallied me. But Daspry, who took an interest in such matters,
came to see me, made a study of the affair,
but reached no conclusion.

A few mornings later, the door-bell rang,
and Antoine came to inform me that a gentleman desired to see me. He would not give
his name. I directed Antoine to show him
up. He was a man about forty years of age
with a very dark complexion, lively features,
and whose correct dress, slightly frayed, proclaimed a taste that contrasted strangely with
his rather vulgar manners. Without any pre-
amble, he said to me—in a rough voice that

confirmed my suspicion as to his social position:

"Monsieur, whilst in a café, I picked up a
copy of the *Gil Blas,* and read your article.
It interested me very much.

"Thank you."

"And here I am."

"Ah!"

"Yes, to talk to you. Are all the facts related by you quite correct?"

"Absolutely so."

"Well, in that case, I can, perhaps, give
you some information."

"Very well; proceed."

"No, not yet. First, I must be sure that
the facts are exactly as you have related
them."

"I have given you my word. What further
proof do you want?"

"I must remain alone in this room."

"I do not understand," I said, with surprise.

"It's an idea that occurred to me when
reading your article. Certain details establish an extraordinary coincidence with another case that came under my notice. If I
am mistaken, I shall say nothing more. And

the only means of ascertaining the truth is by my remaining in the room alone.''

What was at the bottom of this proposition? Later, I recalled that the man was exceedingly nervous; but, at the time, although somewhat astonished, I found nothing particularly abnormal about the man or the request he had made. Moreover, my curiosity was aroused; so I replied:

''Very well. How much time do you require?''

''Oh! three minutes—not longer. Three minutes, from now, I will rejoin you.''

I left the room, and went downstairs. I took out my watch. One minute passed. Two minutes. Why did I feel so depressed? Why did those moments appear so solemn and weird? Two minutes and a half. . . . Two minutes and three quarters. Then I heard a pistol shot.

I bounded up the stairs and entered the room. A cry of horror escaped me. In the middle of the room, the man was lying on his left side, motionless. Blood was flowing from a wound in his forehead. Near his hand was a revolver, still smoking.

But, in addition to this frightful spectacle, my attention was attracted by another object.

At two feet from the body, upon the floor, I saw a playing-card. It was the seven of hearts. I picked it up. The lower extremity of each of the seven spots was pierced with a small round hole.

    *   *   *   *   *

A half-hour later, the commissary of police arrived, then the coroner and the chief of the Sûreté, Mon. Dudouis. I had been careful not to touch the corpse. The preliminary inquiry was very brief, and disclosed nothing. There were no papers in the pockets of the deceased; no name upon his clothes; no initial upon his linen; nothing to give any clue to his identity. The room was in the same perfect order as before. The furniture had not been disturbed. Yet this man had not come to my house solely for the purpose of killing himself, or because he considered my place the most convenient one for his suicide! There must have been a motive for his act of despair, and that motive was, no doubt, the result of some new fact ascertained by him during the three minutes that he was alone.

What was that fact? What had he seen? What frightful secret had been revealed to him? There was no answer to these questions.

But, at the last moment, an incident occurred that appeared to us of considerable
importance. As two policemen were raising
the body to place it on a stretcher, the left
hand being thus disturbed, a crumpled card
fell from it. The card bore these words:
"Georges Andermatt, 37 Rue de Berry."

What did that mean? Georges Andermatt
was a rich banker in Paris, the founder and
president.of the Metal Exchange which had
given such an impulse to the metallic indus-
tries in France. He lived in princely style;
was the possessor of numerous automobiles,
coaches, and an expensive racing-stable. His
social affairs were very select, and Madame
Andermatt was noted for her grace and
beauty.

"Can that be the man's name?" I asked.

The chief of the Sûreté leaned over him.

"It is not he. Mon. Andermatt is a thin
man, and slightly grey."

"But why this card?"

"Have you a telephone, monsieur?"

"Yes, in the vestibule. Come with me."

He looked in the directory, and then asked
for number 415.21.

"Is Mon. Andermatt at home? . . . .
Please tell him that Mon. Dudouis wishes him
to come at once to 102 Boulevard Maillot.
Very important."

Twenty minutes later, Mon. Andermatt arrived in his automobile. After the circumstances had been explained to him, he was
taken in to see the corpse. He displayed considerable emotion, and spoke, in a low tone,
and apparently unwillingly:

"Etienne Varin," he said.

"You know him?"

"No . . . . or, at least, yes . . . . by
sight only. His brother. . . .

"Ah! he has a brother?"

"Yes, Alfred Varin. He came to see me
once on some matter of business. . . . I
forget what it was."

"Where does he live?"

"The two brothers live together—rue de
Provence, I think."

"Do you know any reason why he should
commit suicide?"

"None."

"He held a card in his hand. It was your
card with your address."

"I do not understand that. It must have

been there by some chance that will be disclosed by the investigation.''

A very strange chance, I thought; and I
felt that the others entertained the same impression.

I discovered the same impression in the
papers next day, and amongst all my friends
with whom I discussed the affair. Amid the
mysteries that enveloped it, after the double
discovery of the seven of hearts pierced with
seven holes, after the two inscrutable events
that had happened in my house, that visiting
card promised to throw some light on the affair. Through it, the truth may be revealed.
But, contrary to our expectations, Mon. Andermatt furnished no explanation. He said:

''I have told you all I know. What more
can I do? I am greatly surprised that my
card should be found in such a place, and I
sincerely hope the point will be cleared up.''

It was not. The official investigation established that the Varin brothers were of Swiss
origin, had led a shifting life under various
names, frequenting gambling resorts, associ-
ating with a band of foreigners who had been
dispersed by the police after a series of rob-
beries in which their participation was established only by their flight. At number 24 rue

de Provence, where the Varin brothers had
lived six years before, no one knew what had
become of them.

I confess that, for my part, the case seemed
to me so complicated and so mysterious that
I did not think the problem would ever be
solved, so I concluded to waste no more time
upon it. But Jean Daspry, whom I frequently met at that period, became more and
more interested in it each day. It was he
who pointed out to me that item from a foreign newspaper which was reproduced and
commented upon by the entire press. It was
as follows:

"The first trial of a new model of sub-
marine boat, which is expected to revolution-
ize naval warfare, will be given in presence
of the Emperor at a place that will be kept
secret until the last minute. An indiscretion
has revealed its name; it is called *The Seven-
of-Hearts.*"

The Seven-of-Hearts! That presented a
new problem. Could a connection be established between the name of the sub-marine
and the incidents which we have related?
But a connection of what nature? What had
happened here could have no possible relation
with the sub-marine.

"What do you know about it?" said Daspry to me. "The most diverse effects often proceed from the same cause."

Two days later, the following foreign news item was received and published:

"It is said that the plans of the new submarine *Seven-of-Hearts* were prepared by French engineers, who, having sought, in vain, the support of their compatriots, subsequently entered into negotiations with the British Admiralty, without success."

I do not wish to give undue publicity to certain delicate matters which once provoked considerable excitement. Yet, since all danger of injury therefrom has now come to an end, I must speak of the article that appeared in the *Echo de France,* which aroused so much comment at that time, and which threw considerable light upon the mystery of the Seven-of-Hearts. This is the article as it was published over the signature of Salvator:

"THE AFFAIR OF THE SEVEN-OF-HEARTS.

"A CORNER OF THE VEIL RAISED.

"We will be brief. Ten years ago, a young mining engineer, Louis Lacombe, wishing to devote his time and fortune to certain studies, resigned his position he then held, and rented

number 102 boulevard Maillot, a small house
that had been recently built and decorated
for an Italian count. Through the agency of
the Varin brothers of Lausanne, one of whom
assisted in the preliminary experiments and
the other acted as financial agent, the young
engineer was introduced to Georges Andermatt, the founder of the Metal Exchange.

"After several interviews, he succeeded in
interesting the banker in a sub-marine boat
on which he was working, and it was agreed
that as soon as the invention was perfected,
Mon. Andermatt would use his influence with
the Minister of Marine to obtain a series of
trials under the direction of the government.
For two years, Louis Lacombe was a fre-
quent visitor at Andermatt's house, and he
submitted to the banker the various improve-
ments he made upon his original plans, until
one day, being satisfied with the perfection
of his work, he asked Mon. Andermatt to communicate with the Minister of Marine. That
day, Louis Lacombe dined at Mon. Andermatt's house. He left there about half-past
eleven at night. He has not been seen since.

"A perusal of the newspapers of that date
will show that the young man's family caused
every possible inquiry to be made, but with-

out success; and it was the general opinion
that Louis Lacombe—who was known as an
original and visionary youth—had quietly
left for parts unknown.

"Let us accept that theory—improbable,
though it be,—and let us consider another
question, which is a most important one for
our country: What has become of the plans
of the sub-marine? Did Louis Lacombe carry
they away? Are they destroyed?

"After making a thorough investigation,
we are able to assert, positively, that the
plans are in existence, and are now in the
possession of the two brothers Varin. How
did they acquire such possession? That is
a question not yet determined; nor do we
know why they have not tried to sell them at
an earlier date. Did they fear that their title
to them would be called in question? If so,
they have lost that fear, and we can announce
definitely, that the plans of Louis Lacombe
are now the property of a foreign power,
and we are in a position to publish the correspondence that passed between the Varin
brothers and the representative of that
power. The *Seven-of-Hearts* invented by
Louis Lacombe has been actually constructed
by our neighbor.

"Will the invention fulfil the optimistic expectations of those who were concerned in that treacherous act?"

And a post-script adds:

"Later.—Our special correspondent informs us that the preliminary trial of the *Seven-of-Hearts* has not been satisfactory. It is quite likely that the plans sold and delivered by the Varin brothers did not include the final document carried by Louis Lacombe to Mon. Andermatt on the day of his disappearance, a document that was indispensable to a thorough understanding of the invention. It contained a summary of the final conclusions of the inventor, and estimates and figures not contained in the other papers. Without this document, the plans are incomplete; on the other hand, without the plans, the document is worthless.

"Now is the time to act and recover what belongs to us. It may be a difficult matter, but we rely upon the assistance of Mon. Andermatt. It will be to his interest to explain his conduct which has hitherto been so strange and inscrutable. He will explain not only why he concealed these facts at the time of the suicide of Etienne Varin, but also why he has never revealed the disappearance of

the paper—a fact well known to him. He
will tell why, during the last six years, he
paid spies to watch the movements of the
Varin brothers. We expect from him, not
only words, but acts. And at once. Otherwise——"

The threat was plainly expressed. But of
what did it consist? What whip was Salvator, the anonymous writer of the article,
holding over the head of Mon. Andermatt?

An army of reporters attacked the banker,
and ten interviewers announced the scornful
manner in which they were treated. Thereupon, the *Echo de France* announced its
position in these words:

"Whether Mon. Andermatt is willing or
not, he will be, henceforth, our collaborator
in the work we have undertaken."

*   *   *   *   *

Daspry and I were dining together on the
day on which that announcement appeared.
That evening, with the newspapers spread
over my table, we discussed the affair and
examined it from every point of view with
that exasperation that a person feels when
walking in the dark and finding himself constantly falling over the same obstacles. Suddenly, without any warning whatever, the

door opened and a lady entered. Her face was hidden behind a thick veil. I rose at once and approached her.

"Is it you, monsieur, who lives here?" she asked.

"Yes, madame, but I do not understand—"

"The gate was not locked," she explained.

"But the vestibule door?"

She did not reply, and it occurred to me that she had used the servants' entrance. How did she know the way? Then there was a silence that was quite embarrassing. She looked at Daspry, and I was obliged to introduce him. I asked her to be seated and explain the object of her visit. She raised her veil, and I saw that she was a brunette with regular features and, though not handsome, she was attractive—principally, on account of her sad, dark eyes.

"I am Madame Andermatt," she said.

"Madame Andermatt!" I repeated, with astonishment.

After a brief pause, she continued with a voice and manner that were quite easy and natural:

"I have come to see you about that affair —you know. I thought I might be able to obtain some information——"

"Mon Dieu, madame, I know nothing but what has already appeared in the papers. But if you will point out in what way I can help you. . . ."

"I do not know. . . . I do not know."

Not until then did I suspect that her calm demeanor was assumed, and that some poignant grief was concealed beneath that air of tranquillity. For a moment, we were silent and embarrassed. Then Daspry stepped forward, and said:

"Will you permit me to ask you a few questions?"

"Yes, yes," she cried. "I will answer."

"You will answer . . . . whatever those questions may be?"

"Yes."

"Did you know Louis Lacombe?" he asked.

"Yes, through my husband."

"When did you see him for the last time?"

"The evening he dined with us."

"At that time, was there anything to lead you to believe that you would never see him again?"

"No. But he had spoken of a trip to Russia—in a vague way."

"Then you expected to see him again?"

"Yes. He was to dine with us, two days later."

"How do you explain his disappearance?"

"I cannot explain it."

"And Mon. Andermatt?"

"I do not know."

"Yet the article published in the *Echo de France* indicates——"

"Yes, that the Varin brothers had something to do with his disappearance."

"Is that your opinion?"

"Yes."

"On what do you base your opinion?"

"When he left our house, Louis Lacombe carried a satchel containing all the papers relating to his invention. Two days later, my husband, in a conversation with one of the Varin brothers, learned that the papers were in their possession."

"And he did not denounce them?"

"No."

"Why not?"

"Because there was something else in the satchel—something besides the papers of Louis Lacombe."

"What was it?"

She hesitated; was on the point of speak-

ing, but, finally, remained silent. Daspry
continued:

"I presume that is why your husband has
kept a close watch over their movements instead of informing the police. He hoped to
recover the papers and, at the same time,
that compromising article which has enabled
the two brothers to hold over him threats of
exposure and blackmail."

"Over him, and over me."

"Ah! over you, also?"

"Over me, in particular."

She uttered the last words in a hollow
voice. Daspry observed it; he paced to and
fro for a moment, then, turning to her, asked:

"Had you written to Louis Lacombe?"

"Of course. My husband had business
with him——"

"Apart from those business letters, had
you written to Louis Lacombe . . . . other
letters? Excuse my insistence, but it is absolutely necessary that I should know the truth.
Did you write other letters?"

"Yes," she replied, blushing.

"And those letters came into the possession of the Varin brothers?"

"Yes."

"Does Mon. Andermatt know it?"

"He has not seen them, but Alfred Varin has told him of their existence and threatened to publish them if my husband should take any steps against him. My husband was afraid . . . . of a scandal."

"But he has tried to recover the letters?"

"I think so; but I do not know. You see, after that last interview with Alfred Varin, and after some harsh words between me and my husband in which he called me to account—we live as strangers."

"In that case, as you have nothing to lose, what do you fear?"

"I may be indifferent to him now, but I am the woman that he has loved, the one he would still love—oh! I am quite sure of that," she murmured, in a fervent voice, "he would still love me if he had not got hold of those cursed letters——"

"What! Did he succeed? . . . . But the two brothers still defied him?"

"Yes, and they boasted of having a secure hiding-place."

"Well?"

"I believe my husband has discovered that hiding-place."

"Ah! where was it?"

"Here."

"Here!" I cried, in alarm.

"Yes. I always had that suspicion. Louis Lacombe was very ingenious and amused himself in his leisure hours, by making safes and locks. No doubt, the Varin brothers were aware of that fact and utilized one of Lacombe's safes in which to conceal the letters . . . . and other things, perhaps."

"But they did not live here," I said.

"Before you came, four months ago, the house had been vacant for some time. And they may have thought that your presence here would not interfere with them when they wanted to get the papers. But they did not count on my husband, who came here on the night of 22 June, forced the safe, took what he was seeking, and left his card to inform the two brothers that he feared them no more, and that their positions were now reversed. Two days later, after reading the article in the *Gil Blas*, Etienne Varin came here, remained alone in this room, found the safe empty, and . . . . killed himself."

After a moment, Daspry said:

"A very simple theory. . . . Has Mon. Andermatt spoken to you since then?"

"No."

"Has his attitude toward you changed in

any way? Does he appear more gloomy, more anxious?''

''No, I haven't noticed any change.''

''And yet you think he has secured the letters. Now, in my opinion, he has not got those letters, and it was not he who came here on the night of 22 June.''

''Who was it, then?''

''The mysterious individual who is managing this affair, who holds all the threads in his hands, and whose invisible but far-reaching power we have felt from the beginning. It was he and his friends who entered this house on 22 June; it was he who discovered the hiding-place of the papers; it was he who left Mon. Andermatt's card; it is he who now holds the correspondence and the evidence of the treachery of the Varin brothers.''

''Who is he?'' I asked, impatiently.

''The man who writes letters to the *Echo de France* . . . . Salvator! Have we not convincing evidence of that fact? Does he not mention in his letters certain details that no one could know, except the man who had thus discovered the secrets of the two brothers?''

''Well, then,'' stammered Madame Ander-

matt, in great alarm, "he has my letters also,
and it is he who now threatens my husband.
Mon Dieu! What am I to do?"

"Write to him," declared Daspry. "Confide in him without reserve. Tell him all you
know and all you may hereafter learn. Your
interest and his are the same. He is not
working against Mon. Andermatt, but against
Alfred Varin. Help him."

"How?"

"Has your husband the document that
completes the plans of Louis Lacombe?"

"Yes."

"Tell that to Salvator, and, if possible,
procure the document for him. Write to him
at once. You risk nothing."

The advice was bold, dangerous even at
first sight, but Madame Andermatt had no
choice. Besides, as Daspry had said, she ran
no risk. If the unknown writer were an
enemy, that step would not aggravate the situation. If he were a stranger seeking to
accomplish a particular purpose, he would
attach to those letters only a secondary importance. Whatever might happen, it was
the only solution offered to her, and she, in
her anxiety, was only too glad to act on it.

She thanked us effusively, and promised to
keep us informed.

In fact, two days later, she sent us the
following letter that she had received from
Salvator:

·"Have not found the letters, but I will get
them. Rest easy. I am watching everything. S."

I looked at the letter. It was in the same
handwriting as the note I found in my book
on the night of 22 June.

Daspry was right. Salvator was, indeed,
the originator of that affair.

*   *   *   *   *

We were beginning to see a little light
coming out of the darkness that surrounded
us, and an unexpected light was thrown on
certain points; but other points yet remained
obscure—for instance, the finding of the two
seven-of-hearts. Perhaps I was unnecessa-
rily concerned about those two cards whose
seven punctured spots had, appeared to me
under such startling circumstances! Yet I
could not refrain from asking myself: What
rôle will they play in the drama? What importance do they bear? What conclusion
must be drawn from the fact that the sub-
marine constructed from the plans of Louis

Lacombe bore the name of *Seven-of-Hearts?*

Daspry gave little thought to the two cards; he devoted all his attention to another problem which he considered more urgent; he was seeking the famous hiding-place.

"And who knows," said he, "I may find the letters that Salvator did not find—by inadvertence, perhaps. It is improbable that the Varin brothers would have removed from a spot, which they deemed inacessible, the weapon which was so valuable to them."

And he continued to search. In a short time, the large room held no more secrets for him, so he extended his investigations to the other rooms. He examined the interior and the exterior, the stones of the foundation, the bricks in the walls; he raised the slates of the roof.

One day, he came with a pickaxe and a spade, gave me the spade, kept the pickaxe, pointed to the adjacent vacant lots, and said: "Come."

I followed him, but I lacked his enthusiasm. He divided the vacant land into several sections which he examined in turn. At last, in a corner, at the angle formed by the walls of two neighboring proprietors, a small pile of earth and gravel, covered with briers and

grass, attracted his attention. He attacked
it. I was obliged to help him. For an hour,
under a hot sun, we labored without success.
I was discouraged, but Daspry urged me on.
His ardor was as strong as ever.

At last, Daspry's pickaxe unearthed some
bones—the remains of a skeleton to which
some scraps of clothing still hung. Suddenly,
I turned pale. I had discovered, sticking
in the earth, a small piece of iron cut in the
form of a rectangle, on which I thought I
could see red spots. I stooped and picked it
up. That little iron plate was the exact size
of a playing-card, and the red spots, made
with red lead, were arranged upon it in a
manner similar to the seven of hearts, and
each spot was pierced with a round hole similar to the perforations in the two playing-
cards.

"Listen, Daspry, I have had enough of
this. You can stay, if it interests you. But
I am going."

Was that simply the expression of my excited nerves? Or was it the result of a la-
borious task executed under a burning sun?
I know that I trembled as I walked away,
and that I went to bed, where I remained
forty-eight hours, restless and feverish,

haunted by skeletons that danced around me and threw their bleeding hearts at my head.

Daspry was faithful to me. He came to my house every day, and remained three or four hours, which he spent in the large room, ferreting, thumping, tapping.

"The letters are here, in this room," he said, from time to time, "they are here. I will stake my life on it."

On the morning of the third day I arose—feeble yet, but cured. A substantial breakfast cheered me up. But a letter that I received that afternoon contributed, more than anything else, to my complete recovery, and aroused in me a lively curiosity. This was the letter:

"Monsieur,

"The drama, the first act of which transpired on the night of 22 June, is now drawing to a close. Force of circumstances compel me to bring the two principal actors in that drama face to face, and I wish that meeting to take place in your house, if you will be so kind as to give me the use of it for this evening from nine o'clock to eleven. It will be advisable to give your servant leave of absence for the evening, and, perhaps, you will be so kind as to leave the field open to the two adversaries. You will remember that when I visited your house on the night of 22 June, I took excellent care of your property. I feel that I would do you an injustice if I should doubt, for one moment, your absolute discretion in this affair. Your devoted,

"SALVATOR."

I was amused at the facetious tone of his letter and also at the whimsical nature of his request. There was a charming display of confidence and candor in his language, and nothing in the world could have induced me to deceive him or repay his confidence with ingratitude.

I gave my servant a theatre ticket, and he left the house at eight o'clock. A few minutes later, Daspry arrived. I showed him the letter.

"Well?" said he.

"Well, I have left the garden gate unlocked, so anyone can enter."

"And you—are you going away?"

"Not at all. I intend to stay right here."

"But he asks you to go——"

"But I am not going. I will be discreet, but I am resolved to see what takes place."

"Ma foi!" exclaimed Daspry, laughing, "you are right, and I shall stay with you. I shouldn't like to miss it.'"

We were interrupted by the sound of the door-bell.

"Here already?" said Daspry, "twenty minutes ahead of time! Incredible!"

I went to the door and ushered in the visitor. It was Madame Andermatt. She was faint and nervous, and in a stammering voice, she ejaculated:

"My husband . . . . is coming . . . . he has an appointment . . . . they intend to give him the letters. . . ."

"How do you know?" I asked.

"By chance. A message came for my husband while we were at dinner. The servant gave it to me by mistake. My husband grabbed it quickly, but he was too late. I had read it."

"You read it?"

"Yes. It was something like this: *'At nine o'clock this evening, be at Boulevard Maillot with the papers connected with the affair. In exchange, the letters.'* So, after dinner, I hastened here."

"Unknown to your husband?"

"Yes."

"What do you think about it?" asked Daspry, turning to me.

"I think as you do, that Mon. Andermatt is one of the invited guests.'"

"Yes, but for what purpose?"

"That is what we are going to find out."

I led them to the large room. The three of us could hide comfortably behind the velvet chimney-mantle, and observe all that should happen in the room. We seated ourselves there, with Madame Andermatt in the centre.

The clock struck nine. A few minutes later, the garden gate creaked upon its hinges. I confess I was greatly agitated. I was about to learn the key to the mystery. The startling events of the last few weeks were about to be explained, and, under my eyes, the last battle was going to be fought. Daspry seized the hand of Madame Andermatt, and said to her:

"Not a word, not a movement! Whatever you may see or hear, keep quiet!"

Some one entered. It was Alfred Varin. I recognized him at once, owing to the close resemblance he bore to his brother Etienne. There was the same slouching gait; the same cadaverous face covered with a black beard.

He entered with the nervous air of a man
who is accustomed to fear the presence of
traps and ambushes; who scents and avoids
them. He glanced about the room, and I had
the impression that the chimney, masked with
a velvet portière, did not please him. He
took three steps in our direction, when something caused him to turn and walk toward
the old mosaic king, with the flowing beard
and flamboyant sword, which he examined
minutely, mounting on a chair and following
with his finger the outlines of the shoulders
and head and feeling certain parts of the face.
Suddenly, he leaped from the chair and
walked away from it. He had heard the
sound of approaching footsteps. Mon.
Andermatt appeared at the door.

"You! You!" exclaimed the banker.
"Was it you who brought me here?"

"I? By no means," protested Varin, in
a rough, jerky voice that reminded me of his
brother, "on the contrary, it was your letter
that brought me here."

"My letter?"

"A letter signed by you, in which you
offered——"

"I never wrote to you," declared Mon.
Andermatt.

"You did not write to me!"

Instinctively, Varin was put on his guard, not against the banker, but against the unknown enemy who had drawn him into this trap. A second time, he looked in our direction, then walked toward the door. But Mon. Andermatt barred his passage.

"Well, where are you going, Varin?"

"There is something about this affair I don't like. I am going home. Good evening."

"One moment!"

"No need of that, Mon. Andermatt. I have nothing to say to you."

"But I have something to say to you, and this is a good time to say it."

"Let me pass."

"No, you will not pass."

Varin recoiled before the resolute attitude of the banker, as he muttered:

"Well, then, be quick about it."

One thing astonished me; and I have no doubt my two companions experienced a similar feeling. Why was Salvator not there? Was he not a necessary party at this conference? Or was he satisfied to let these two adversaries fight it out between themselves? At all events, his absence was a great disap-

pointment, although it did not detract from
the dramatic strength of the situation.

After a moment, Mon. Andermatt approached Varin and, face to face, eye to eye,
said:

"Now, after all these years and when you
have nothing more to fear, you can answer
me candidly: What have you done with Louis
Lacombe?"

"What a question! As if I knew anything
about him!"

"You do know! You and your brother
were his constant companions, almost lived
with him in this very house. You knew all
about his plans and his work. And the last
night I ever saw Louis Lacombe, when I
parted with him at my door, I saw two men
slinking away in the shadows of the trees.
That, I am ready to swear to."

"Well, what has that to do with me?"

"The two men were you and your
brother."

"Prove it."

"The best proof is that, two days later, you
yourself showed me the papers and the plans
that belonged to Lacombe and offered to sell
them. How did those papers come into your
possession?"

"I have already told you, Mon. Andermatt,

that we found them on Louis Lacombe's table, the morning after his disappearance.''

"That is a lie!''

"Prove it."

"The law will prove it."

"Why did you not appeal to the law?''

"Why? Ah! Why——,'' stammered the banker, with a slight display of emotion.

"You know very well, Mon. Andermatt, if you had had the least certainty of our guilt, our little threat would not have stopped you."

"What threat? Those letters? Do you suppose I ever gave those letters a moment's thought?''

"If you did not care for the letters, why did you offer me thousands of francs for their return? And why did you have my brother and me tracked like wild beasts?''

"To recover the plans."

"Nonsense! You wanted the letters. You knew that as soon as you had the letters in your possession, you could denounce us. Oh! no, I couldn't part with them!''

He laughed heartily, but stopped suddenly, and said:

"But, enough of this! We are merely going over the old ground. We make no head-

way. We had better let things stand as they
are.''

''We will not let them stand as they are,''
said the banker, ''and since you have referred
to the letters, let me tell you that you will not
leave this house until you deliver up those
letters.''

''I shall go when I please.''

''You will not.''

''Be careful, Mon. Andermatt. I warn
you——''

''I say, you shall not go.''

''We will see about that,'' cried Varin, in
such a rage that Madame Andermatt could
not suppress a cry of fear. Varin must have
heard it, for he now tried to force his way
out. Mon. Andermatt pushed him back. Then
I saw him put his hand into his coat pocket.

''For the last time, let me pass,'' he cried.

''The letters, first!''

Varin drew a revolver and, pointing it at
Mon. Andermatt, said:

''Yes or no?''

The banker stooped quickly. There was
the sound of a pistol-shot. The weapon fell
from Varin's hand. I was amazed. The shot
was fired close to me. It was Daspry who
had fired it at Varin, causing him to drop the

revolver. In a moment, Daspry was standing between the two men, facing Varin; he said to him, with a sneer:

"You were lucky, my friend, very lucky. I fired at your hand and struck only the revolver."

Both of them looked at him, surprised. Then he turned to the banker, and said:

"I beg your pardon, monsieur, for meddling in your business; but, really, you play a very poor game. Let me hold the cards."

Turning again to Varin, Daspry said:

"It's between us two, comrade, and play fair, if you please. Hearts are trumps, and I play the seven."

Then Daspry held up, before Varin's bewildered eyes, the little iron plate, marked with the seven red spots. It was a terrible shock to Varin. With livid features, staring eyes, and an air of intense agony, the man seemed to be hypnotized at the sight of it.

"Who are you?" he gasped.

"One who meddles in other people's business, down to the very bottom."

"What do you want?"

"What you brought here tonight."

"I brought nothing."

"Yes, you did, or you wouldn't have come.

This morning, you received an invitation to come here at nine o'clock, and bring with you all the papers held by you. You are here. Where are the papers?''

There was in Daspry's voice and manner a tone of authority that I did not understand; his manner was usually quite mild and conciliatory. Absolutely conquered, Varin placed his hand on one of his pockets, and said:

''The papers are here.''

''All of them?''

''Yes.''

''All that you took from Louis Lacombe and afterwards sold to Major von Lieben?''

''Yes.''

''Are these the copies or the originals?''

''I have the originals.''

''How much do you want for them?''

''One hundred thousand francs.''

''You are crazy,'' said Daspry. ''Why, the major gave you only twenty thousand, and that was like money thrown into the sea, as the boat was a failure at the preliminary trials.''

''They didn't understand the plans.''

''The plans are not complete.''

''Then, why do you ask me for them?''

''Because I want them. I offer you five

thousand francs—not a sou more.''

''Ten thousand. Not a sou less.''

''Agreed,'' said Daspry, who now turned to Mon. Andermatt, and said:

''Monsieur will kindly sign a check for the amount.''

''But . . . . I haven't got——''

''Your check-book? Here it is.''

Astounded, Mon. Andermatt examined the check-book that Daspry had handed to him.

''It is mine,'' he gasped. ''How does that happen?''

''No idle words, monsieur, if you please. You have merely to sign.''

The banker took out his fountain pen, filled out the check and signed it. Varin held out his hand for it.

''Put down your hand,'' said Daspry, ''there is something more.'' Then, to the banker, he said: ''You asked for some letters, did you not?''

''Yes, a package of letters.''

''Where are they, Varin?''

''I haven't got them.''

''Where are they, Varin?''

''I don't know. My brother had charge of them.''

"They are hidden in this room."

"In that case, you know where they are."

"How should I know?"

"Was it not you who found the hiding-place? You appear to be as well informed . . . . as Salvator."

"The letters are not in the hiding-place."

"They are."

"Open it."

Varin looked at him, defiantly. Were not Daspry and Salvator the same person? Everything pointed to that conclusion. If so, Varin risked nothing in disclosing a hiding-place already known.

"Open it," repeated Daspry.

"I have not got the seven of hearts."

"Yes, here it is," said Daspry, handing him the iron plate. Varin recoiled in terror, and cried:

"No, no, I will not."

"Never mind," replied Daspry, as he walked toward the bearded king, climbed on a chair and applied the seven of hearts to the lower part of the sword in such a manner that the edges of the iron plate coincided exactly with the two edges of the sword. Then, with the assistance of an awl which he introduced alternately into each of the seven holes, he pressed upon seven of the little mosaic stones. As he pressed upon the seventh one, a clicking sound was heard, and the entire bust of the King turned upon a pivot, disclosing a large opening lined with steel. It was really a fire-proof safe.

"You can see, Varin, the safe is empty."

"So I see. Then, my brother has taken out the letters."

Daspry stepped down from the chair, approached Varin, and said:

"Now, no more nonsense with me. There is another hiding-place. Where is it?"

"There is none."

"Is it money you want? How much?"

"Ten thousand."

"Monsieur Andermatt, are those letters worth ten thousand francs to you?"

"Yes," said the banker, firmly.

Varin closed the safe, took the seven of hearts and placed it again on the sword at the same spot. He thrust the awl into each of the seven holes. There was the same clicking sound, but this time, strange to relate, it was only a portion of the safe that revolved on the pivot, disclosing quite a small safe that was built within the door of the larger one. The packet of letters was there, tied

with a tape, and sealed. Varin handed the
packet to Daspry. The latter turned to the
banker, and asked:

"Is the check ready, Monsieur Andermatt?"

"Yes."

"And you have also the last document that
you received from Louis Lacombe—the one
that completes the plans of the sub-marine?"

"Yes."

The exchange was made. Daspry pocketed
the document and the checks, and offered the
packet of letters to Mon. Andermatt.

"This is what you wanted, Monsieur."

The banker hesitated a moment, as if he
were afraid to touch those cursed letters that
he had sought so eagerly. Then, with a
nervous movement, he took them. Close to
me, I heard a moan. I grasped Madame
Andermatt's hand. It was cold.

"I believe, monsieur," said Daspry to the
banker, "that our business is ended. Oh!
no thanks. It was only by a mere chance that
I have been able to do you a good turn. Good-
night."

Mon. Andermatt retired. He carried with
him the letters written by his wife to Louis
Lacombe.

"Marvelous!" exclaimed Daspry, delighted. "Everything is coming our way. Now, we have only to close our little affair, comrade. You have the papers?"

"Here they are—all of them."

Daspry examined them carefully, and then placed them in his pocket.

"Quite right. You have kept your word," he said.

"But——"

"But what?"

"The two checks? The money?" said Varin, eagerly.

"Well, you have a great deal of assurance, my man. How dare you ask such a thing?"

"I ask only what is due me."

"Can you ask pay for returning papers that you stole? Well, I think not!"

Varin was beside himself. He trembled with rage; his eyes were bloodshot.

"The money . . . . the twenty thousand . . . ." he stammered.

"Impossible! I need it myself."

"The money!"

"Come, be reasonable, and don't get excited. It won't do you any good."

Daspry seized his arm so forcibly, that

Varin uttered a cry of pain. Daspry continued:

"Now, you can go. The air will do you
good. Perhaps you want me to show you the
way. Ah! yes, we will go together to the vacant lot near here, and I will show you a little mound of earth and stones and under
it——"

"That is false! That is false!"

"Oh! no, it is true. That little iron plate
with the seven spots on it came from there.
Louis Lacombe always carried it, and you
buried it with the body—and with some other
things that will prove very interesting to a
judge and jury."

Varin covered his face with his hands, and
muttered:

"All right, I am beaten. Say no more. But
I want to ask you one question. I should like
to know——"

"What is it?"

"Was there a little casket in the large
safe?"

"Yes."

"Was it there on the night of 22 June?"

"Yes."

"What did it contain?"

"Everything that the Varin brothers had

put in it—a very pretty collection of diamonds and pearls picked up here and there
by the said brothers.''

"And did you take it?"

"Of course I did. Do you blame me?"

"I understand. . . . it was the disappearance of that casket that caused my brother to
kill himself.''

"Probably. The disappearance of your
correspondence was not a sufficient motive.
But the disappearance of the casket. . . . Is
that all you wish to ask me?"

"One thing more: your name?"

"You ask that with an idea of seeking revenge.''

"Parbleu! The tables may be turned. To-
day, you are on top. To-morrow——''

"It will be you.''

"I hope so. Your name?"

"Arsène Lupin.''

"Arsène Lupin!''

The man staggered, as though stunned by
a heavy blow. Those two words had deprived
him of all hope.

Daspry laughed, and said:

"Ah! did you imagine that a Monsieur
Durand or Dupont could manage an affair
like this? No, it required the skill and cun-

ning of Arsène Lupin. And now that you
have my name, go and prepare your revenge.
Arsène Lupin will wait for you.''

Then he pushed the bewildered Varin
through the door.

''Daspry! Daspry!'' I cried, pushing aside
the curtain. He ran to me.

''What? What's the matter?''

''Madame Andermatt is ill.''

He hastened to her, caused her to inhale
some salts, and, while caring for her, questioned me:

''Well, what did it?''

''The letters of Louis Lacombe that you
gave to her husband.''

He struck his forehead and said:

''Did she think that I could do such a
thing! . . . But, of course she would. Imbecile that I am!''

Madame Andermatt was now revived. Daspry took from his pocket a small package exactly similar to the one that Mon. Andermatt
had carried away.

''Here are your letters, Madame. These
are the genuine letters.''

''But . . . . the others?''

''The others are the same, rewritten by me
and carefully worded. Your husband will

not find anything objectionable in them, and will never suspect the substitution since they were taken from the safe in his presence."

"But the handwriting——"

"There is no handwriting that cannot be imitated."

She thanked him in the same words she might have used to a man in her own social circle, so I concluded she had not witnessed the final scene between Varin and Arsène Lupin. But the surprising revelation caused me considerable embarrassment. Lupin! My club companion was none other than Arsène Lupin. I could not realize it. But he said, quite at his ease:

"You can say farewell to Jean Daspry."

"Ah!"

"Yes, Jean Daspry is going on a long journey. I shall send him to Morocco. There, he may find a death worthy of him. I may say that that is his expectation."

"But Arsène Lupin will remain?"

"Oh! Decidedly. Arsène Lupin is simply at the threshold of his career, and he expects——"

I was impelled by curiosity to interrupt him, and, leading him away from the hearing of Madame Andermatt, I asked:

"Did you discover the smaller safe yourself—the one that held the letters?"

"Yes, after a great deal of trouble. I
found it yesterday afternoon while you were
asleep. And yet, God knows it was simple
enough! But the simplest things are the ones
that usually escape our notice." Then, show-
ing me the seven-of-hearts, he added: "Of
course I had guessed that, in order to open
the larger safe, this card must be placed on
the sword of the mosaic king.

"How did you guess that?"

"Quite easily. Through private information, I knew that fact when I came here on
the evening of 22 June——"

"After you left me——"

"Yes, after turning the subject of our conversation to stories of crime and robbery
which were sure to reduce you to such a
nervous condition that you would not leave
your bed, but would allow me to complete my
search uninterrupted."

"The scheme worked perfectly."

"Well, I knew when I came here that there
was a casket concealed in a safe with a secret
lock, and that the seven of hearts was the key
to that lock. I had merely to place the card
upon the spot that was obviously intended

for it. An hour's examination showed me where that spot was.''

"One hour!''

"Observe the fellow in mosaic.''

"The old emperor?''

"That old emperor is an exact representation of the king of hearts on all playing-cards.''

"That's right. But how does the seven of hearts open the larger safe at one time and the smaller safe at another time? And why did you open only the larger safe in the first instance? I mean on the night of 22 June.''

"Why? Because I always placed the seven of hearts in the same way. I never changed the position. But, yesterday, I observed that by reversing the card, by turning it upside down, the arrangement of the seven spots on the mosaic were changed.''

"Parbleu!''

"Of course, parbleu! But a person has to think of those things.''

"There is something else: you did not know the history of those letters until Madame Andermatt——''

"Spoke of them before me? No. Because I found in the safe, besides the casket, nothing but the correspondence of the two broth-

ers which disclosed their treachery in regard
to the plans.''

''Then it was by chance that you were led,
first, to investigate the history of the two
brothers, and then to search for the plans and
documents relating to the submarine?''

''Simply by chance.''

''For what purpose did you make the
search?''

''Mon Dieu!'' exclaimed Daspry, laughing,
''how deeply interested you are!''

''The subject fascinates me.''

''Very well, presently, after I have escorted Madame Andermatt to a carriage, and
dispatched a short story to the *Echo de
France,* I will return and tell you all about
it.''

He sat down and wrote one of those short,
clear-cut articles which served to amuse and
mystify the public. Who does not recall the
sensation that the following article produced
throughout the entire world?

''Arsène Lupin has solved the problem recently submitted by Salvator. Having acquired possession of all the documents and
original plans of the engineer Louis Lacombe, he has placed them in the hands of the
Minister of Marine, and he has headed a sub-

scription list for the purpose of presenting to the nation the first submarine constructed from those plans. His subscription is twenty thousand francs."

"Twenty thousand francs! The checks of Mon. Andermatt?" I exclaimed, when he had given me the paper to read.

"Exactly. It was quite right that Varin should redeem his treachery."

* * * * *

And that is how I made the acquaintance of Arsène Lupin. That is how I learned that Jean Daspry, a member of my club, was none other than Arsène Lupin, gentleman-thief. That is how I formed very agreeable ties of friendship with that famous man, and, thanks to the confidence with which he honored me, how I became his very humble and faithful historiographer.

Chapter VII

T three o'clock in the morning, there were still half-a-dozen carriages in front of one of those small houses which form the only side of the boulevard Berthier. The door of that house opened, and a number of guests, male and female, emerged. The majority of them entered their carriages and were quickly driven away, leaving behind only two men who walked down the boulevard together as far as the rue de Courcelles, where they parted, as one of them lived in that street. The other decided to return on foot as far as the Porte-Maillot. It was a beautiful winter's night, clear and cold; a night on which a brisk walk is agreeable and refreshing.

But, at the end of a few minutes, he had the disagreeable impression that he was being followed. Turning around, he saw a man skulking amongst the trees. He was not a coward; yet he felt it advisable to increase his speed. Then his pursuer commenced to

run; and he deemed it prudent to draw his
revolver and face him. But he had no time.
The man rushed at him and attacked him vio-
lently. Immediately, they were engaged in
a desperate struggle, wherein he felt that his
unknown assailant had the advantage. He
called for help, struggled, and was thrown
down on a pile of gravel, seized by the throat,
and gagged with a handkerchief that his assailant forced into his mouth. His eyes
closed, his ears buzzed, and he was losing
consciousness when, suddenly, the pressure
relaxed, and the man who was smothering
him with his weight arose to defend himself
against an unexpected attack. A blow from
a cane and a kick from a boot; the man uttered two cries of pain, and fled, limping and
cursing. Without deigning to pursue the
fugitive, the new arrival stooped over the
prostrate man and inquired:

"Are you hurt, monsieur?"

He was not injured, but he was dazed and
unable to stand. His rescuer procured a
carriage, placed him in it, and accompanied
him to his house on the avenue de la Grande-
Armée. On his arrival there, quite recovered, he overwhelmed his saviour with thanks.

"I owe you my life, monsieur, and I shall

not forget it. I do not wish to alarm my
wife at this time of night, but, to-morrow,
she will be pleased to thank you personally.
Come and breakfast with us. My name is
Ludovic Imbert. May I ask yours?"

"Certainly, monsieur."

And he handed Mon. Imbert a card bearing
the name: "Arsène Lupin."

*   *   *   *   *

At that time, Arsène Lupin did not enjoy
the celebrity which the Cahorn affair, his
escape from the Prison de la Santé, and other
brilliant exploits, afterwards gained for him.
He had not even used the name of Arsène
Lupin. The name was specially invented to
designate the rescuer of Mon. Imbert; that
is to say, it was in that affair that Arsène
Lupin was baptized. Fully armed and ready
for the fray, it is true, but lacking the resources and authority which command success, Arsène Lupin was then merely an ap-
prentice in a profession wherein he soon became a master.

With what a thrill of joy he recalled the
invitation he had received that night! At
last, he had reached his goal! At last, he had
undertaken a task worthy of his strength and

skill! The Imbert millions! What a magnificent feast for an appetite like his!

He prepared a special toilet for the occasion; a shabby frock-coat, baggy trousers, a
frayed silk hat, well-worn collar and cuffs, all
quite correct in form, but bearing the unmis-
takable stamp of poverty. His cravat was a
black ribbon pinned with a false diamond.
Thus accoutred, he descended the stairs of
the house in which he lived at Montmartre.
At the third floor, without stopping, he
rapped on a closed door with the head of
his cane. He walked to the exterior boulevards. A tram-car was passing. He boarded
it, and some one who had been following him
took a seat beside him. It was the lodger
who occupied the room on the third floor. A
moment later, this man said to Lupin:

"Well, governor?"

"Well, it is all fixed."

"How?"

"I am going there to breakfast."

"You breakfast—there!"

"Certainly. Why not? I rescued Mon.
Ludovic Imbert from certain death at your
hands. Mon. Imbert is not devoid of gratitude. He has invited me to breakfast."

There was a brief silence. Then the other said:

"But you are not going to throw up the scheme?"

"My dear boy," said Lupin, "when I arranged that little case of assault and battery, when I took the trouble at three o'clock in the morning, to rap you with my cane and tap you with my boot at the risk of injuring my only friend, it was not my intention to forego the advantages to be gained from a rescue so well arranged and executed. Oh! no, not at all."

"But the strange rumors we hear about their fortune?"

"Never mind about that. For six months, I have worked on this affair, investigated it, studied it, questioned the servants, the money-lenders and men of straw; for six months, I have shadowed the husband and wife. Consequently, I know what I am talking about. Whether the fortune came to them from old Brawford, as they pretend, or from some other source, I do not care. I know that it is a reality; that it exists. And some day it will be mine."

"Bigre! one hundred millions!"

"Let us say ten, or even five—that is

enough! They have a safe full of bonds, and there will be the devil to pay if I can't get my hands on them.''

The tram-car stopped at the Place de l'Etoile. The man whispered to Lupin:

''What am I to do now?''

''Nothing, at present. You will hear from me. There is no hurry.''

Five minutes later, Arsène Lupin was ascending the magnificent flight of stairs in the Imbert mansion, and Mon. Imbert introduced him to his wife. Madame Gervaise Imbert was a short plump woman, and very talkative. She gave Lupin a cordial welcome.

''I desired that we should be alone to entertain our saviour,'' she said.

From the outset, they treated ''our saviour'' as an old and valued friend. By the time dessert was served, their friendship was well cemented, and private confidences were being exchanged. Arsène related the story of his life, the life of his father as a magistrate, the sorrows of his childhood, and his present difficulties. Gervaise, in turn, spoke of her youth, her marriage, the kindness of the aged Brawford, the hundred millions that she had inherited, the obstacles that prevented her from obtaining the enjoyment of

her inheritance, the moneys she had been
obliged to borrow at an exorbitant rate of interest, her endless contentions with Brawford's nephews, and the litigation! the in-
junctions! in fact, everything!

"Just think of it, Monsieur Lupin, the
bonds are there, in my husband's office, and
if we detach a single coupon, we lose everything! They are there, in our safe, and we
dare not touch them."

Monsieur Lupin shivered at the bare idea
of his proximity to so much wealth. Yet he
felt quite certain that Monsieur Lupin would
never suffer from the same difficulty as his
fair hostess who declared she dare not touch
the money.

"Ah! they are there!" he repeated, to
himself; "they are there!"

A friendship formed under such circumstances soon led to closer relations. When
discreetly questioned, Arsène Lupin confessed his poverty and distress. Immediately, the unfortunate young man was appointed
private secretary to the Imberts, husband and
wife, at a salary of one hundred francs a
month. He was to come to the house every
day and receive orders for his work, and a
room on the second floor was set apart as his

office. This room was directly over Mon.
Imbert's office.

Arsène soon realized that his position as
secretary was essentially a sinecure. During
the first two months, he had only four important letters to recopy, and was called only
once to Mon. Imbert's office; consequently,
he had only one opportunity to contemplate,
officially, the Imbert safe. Moreover, he noticed that the secretary was not invited to
the social functions of his employer. But he
did not complain, as he preferred to remain,
modestly, in the shade and maintain his peace
and freedom. However, he was not wasting
any time. From the beginning, he made
clandestine visits to Mon. Imbert's office, and
paid his respects to the safe, which was her-
metically closed. It was an immense block
of iron and steel, cold and stern in appearance, which could not be forced open by the
ordinary tools of the burglar's trade. But
Arsène Lupin was not discouraged.

"Where force fails, cunning prevails," he
said to himself. "The essential thing is to be
on the spot when the opportunity occurs. In
the meantime, I must watch and wait."

He made immediately some preliminary
preparations. After careful soundings made

upon the floor of his room, he introduced a
lead pipe which penetrated to the ceiling of
Mon. Imbert's office at a point between two
screeds of the cornice. By means of this
pipe, he hoped to see and hear what transpired in the room below.

. Henceforth, he passed his days stretched
at full length upon the floor. He frequently
saw the Imberts holding a consultation in
front of the safe, investigating books and
papers. When they turned the combination
lock, he tried to learn the figures and the
number of turns they made to right and left.
He watched their movements; he sought to
catch their words. There was also a key
necessary to complete the opening of the safe.
What did they do with it? Did they hide it?

One day, he saw them leave the room without locking the safe. He descended the stairs
quickly, and boldly entered the room. But
they had returned.

"Oh! excuse me," he said, "I made a mistake in the door."

"Come in, Monsieur Lupin, come in," cried
Madame Imbert, "are you not at home here?
We want your advice. What bonds should
we sell? The foreign securities or the government annuities?"

"But the injunction?" said Lupin, with surprise.

"Oh! it doesn't cover all the bonds."

She opened the door of the safe and withdrew a package of bonds. But her husband protested.

"No, no, Gervaise, it would be foolish to sell the foreign bonds. They are going up, whilst the annuities are as high as they ever will be. What do you think, my dear friend?"

The dear friend had no opinion; yet he advised the sacrifice of the annuities. Then she withdrew another package and, from it, she took a paper at random. It proved to be a three-per-cent annuity worth two thousand francs. Ludovic placed the package of bonds in his pocket. That afternoon, accompanied by his secretary, he sold the annuities to a stock-broker and realized forty-six thousand francs.

Whatever Madame Imbert might have said about it, Arsène Lupin did not feel at home in the Imbert house. On the contrary, his position there was a peculiar one. He learned that the servants did not even know his name. They called him "monsieur." Ludovic always spoke of him in the same way: "You

will tell monsieur. Has monsieur arrived?"
Why that mysterious appellation?

Moreover, after their first outburst of enthusiasm, the Imberts seldom spoke to him,
and, although treating him with the consideration due to a benefactor, they gave him
little or no attention. They appeared to regard him as an eccentric character who did
not like to be disturbed, and they respected
his isolation as if it were a stringent rule on
his part. On one occasion, while passing
through the vestibule, he heard Madame
Imbert say to two gentlemen:

"He is such a barbarian!"

"Very well," he said to himself, "I am a
barbarian."

And, without seeking to solve the question
of their strange conduct, he proceeded with
the execution of his own plans. He had decided that he could not depend on chance, nor
on the negligence of Madame Imbert, who
carried the key of the safe, and who, on locking the safe, invariably scattered the letters
forming the combination of the lock. Consequently, he must act for himself.

Finally, an incident precipitated matters;
it was the vehement campaign instituted
against the Imberts by certain newspapers

that accused the Imberts of swindling.
Arsène Lupin was present at certain family
conferences when this new vicissitude was
discussed. He decided that if he waited much
longer, he would lose everything. During the
next five days, instead of leaving the house
about six o'clock, according to his usual habit,
he locked himself in his room. It was supposed that he had gone out. But he was
lying on the floor surveying the office of Mon.
Imbert. During those five evenings, the fa-
vorable opportunity that he awaited did not
take place. He left the house about midnight
by a side door to which he held a key.

But on the sixth day, he learned that the
Imberts, actuated by the malevolent insin-
uations of their enemies, proposed to make
an examination and inventory of the contents
of the safe.

"They will do it to-night," thought Lupin.

And truly, after dinner, Imbert and his
wife retired to the office and commenced to
examine the books of account and the securities contained in the safe. Thus, one hour
after another passed away. He heard the
servants go upstairs to their rooms. No one
now remained on the first floor. Midnight!
The Imberts were still at work.

"I must get to work," murmured Lupin.

He opened his window. It opened on a court. Outside, everything was dark and quiet. He took from his desk a knotted rope, fastened it to the balcony in front of his window, and quietly descended as far as the window below, which was that of Imbert's office. He stood upon the balcony for a moment, motionless, with attentive ear and watchful eye, but the heavy curtains effectually concealed the interior of the room. He cautiously pushed on the double window. If no one had examined it, it ought to yield to the slightest pressure, for, during the afternoon, he had so fixed the bolt that it would not enter the staple.

The window yielded to his touch. Then, with infinite care, he pushed it open sufficiently to admit his head. He parted the curtains a few inches, looked in, and saw Mon. Imbert and his wife sitting in front of the safe, deeply absorbed in their work and speaking softly to each other at rare intervals.

He calculated the distance between him and them, considered the exact movements he would require to make in order to overcome them, one after the other, before they could

call for help, and he was about to rush upon
them, when Madame Imbert said:

"Ah! the room is getting quite cold. I am
going to bed. And you, my dear?"

"I shall stay and finish."

"Finish! Why, that will take you all
night."

"Not at all. An hour, at the most."

She retired. Twenty minutes, thirty minutes passed. Arsène pushed the window a
little farther open. The curtains shook. He
pushed once more. Mon. Imbert turned, and,
seeing the curtains blown by the wind, he
rose to close the window.

There was not a cry, not the trace of a
struggle. With a few precise movements,
and without causing him the least injury,
Arsène stunned him, wrapped the curtain
about his head, bound him hand and foot, and
did it all in such a manner that Mon. Imbert
had no opportunity to recognize his assailant.

Quickly, he approached the safe, seized
two packages that he placed under his arm,
left the office, descended the stairs, crossed
the yard, and opened the servants' gate. A
carriage was stationed in the street.

"Take that, first—and follow me," he said
to the coachman. He returned to the office,

and, in two trips, they emptied the safe. Then
Arsène went to his own room, removed the
rope, and all other traces of his clandestine
work.

A few hours later, Arsène Lupin and his
assistant examined the stolen goods. Lupin
was not disappointed, as he had foreseen that
the wealth of the Imberts had been greatly
exaggerated. It did not consist of hundreds
of millions, nor even tens of millions. Yet it
amounted to a very respectable sum, and
Lupin expressed his satisfaction.

"Of course," he said, "there will be a considerable loss when we come to sell the bonds,
as we will have to dispose of them surrepti-
tiously at reduced prices. In the meantime,
they will rest quietly in my desk awaiting a
propitious moment."

Arsène saw no reason why he should not
go to the Imbert house next day. But a perusal of the morning papers revealed this startling fact: Ludovic and Gervaise Imbert had
disappeared.

When the officers of the law seized the safe
and opened it, they found there what Arsène
Lupin had left—nothing.

*   *   *   *   *

Such are the facts; and I learned the sequel

to them, one day, when Arsène Lupin was in
a confidential mood. He was pacing to and
fro in my room, with a nervous step and a
feverish eye that were unusual to him.

"After all," I said to him, "it was your
most successful venture."

Without making a direct reply, he said:

"There are some impenetrable secrets connected with that affair; some obscure points
that escape my comprehension. For instance:
What caused their flight? Why did they not
take advantage of the help I unconsciously
gave them? It would have been so simple to
say: 'The hundred millions were in the safe.
They are no longer there, because they have
been stolen.'"

"They lost their nerve."

"Yes, that is it—they lost their nerve. . . .
On the other hand, it is true——"

"What is true?"

"Oh! nothing."

What was the meaning of Lupin's reti-
cence? It was quite obvious that he had not
told me everything; there was something he
was loath to tell. His conduct puzzled me. It
must indeed be a very serious matter to cause
such a man as Arsène Lupin even a momen-

tary hesitation. I threw out a few questions at random.

"Have you not seen them since?"

"No."

"And have you never experienced the slightest degree of pity for those unfortunate people?"

"I!" he exclaimed, with a start.

His sudden excitement astonished me. Had I touched him on a sore spot? I continued:

"Of course. If you had left them alone, they might have been able to face the danger, or, at least, made their escape with full pockets."

"What do you mean?" he said, indignantly. "I suppose you have an idea that my soul should be filled with remorse?"

"Call it remorse or regrets—anything you like——"

"They are not worth it."

"Have you no regrets or remorse for having stolen their fortune?"

"What fortune?"

"The packages of bonds you took from their safe."

"Oh! I stole their bonds, did I? I deprived them of a portion of their wealth? Is that my crime? Ah! my dear boy, you do not know

the truth. You never imagined that those
bonds were not worth the paper they were
written on. Those bonds were false—they
were counterfeit—every one of them—do you
understand? THEY WERE COUNTERFEIT!

I looked at him, astounded.

"Counterfeit! The four or five millions?"

"Yes, counterfeit!" he exclaimed, in a fit
of rage. "Only so many scraps of paper! I
couldn't raise a sou on the whole of them!
And you ask me if I have any remorse. *They*
are the ones who should have remorse and
pity. They played me for a simpleton; and
I fell into their trap. I was their latest victim, their most stupid gull!"

He was affected by genuine anger—the result of malice and wounded pride. He continued:

"From start to finish, I got the worst of it.
Do you know the part I played in that affair,
or rather the part they made me play? That
of André Brawford! Yes, my boy, that is the
truth, and I never suspected it. It was not
until afterwards, on reading the newspapers,
that the light dawned in my stupid brain.
Whilst I was posing as his "saviour," as the
gentleman who had risked his life to rescue
Mon. Imbert from the clutches of an assassin,

they were passing me off as Brawford. Wasn't that splendid? That eccentric individual who had a room on the second floor, that barbarian that was exhibited only at a distance, was Brawford, and Brawford was I! Thanks to me, and to the confidence that I inspired under the name of Brawford, they were enabled to borrow money from the bankers and other money-lenders. Ha! what an experience for a novice! And I swear to you that I shall profit by the lesson!"

He stopped, seized my arm, and said to me, in a tone of exasperation:

"My dear fellow, at this very moment, Gervaise Imbert owes me fifteen hundred francs."

I could not refrain from laughter, his rage was so grotesque. He was making a mountain out of a molehill. In a moment, he laughed himself, and said:

"Yes, my boy, fifteen hundred francs. You must know that I had not received one sou of my promised salary, and, more than that, she had borrowed from me the sum of fifteen hundred francs. All my youthful savings! And do you know why? To devote the money to charity! I am giving you a straight story. She wanted it for some poor people she was

assisting—unknown to her husband. And
my hard-earned money was wormed out of
me by that silly pretence! Isn't it amusing,
hein? Arsène Lupin done out of fifteen hundred francs by the fair lady from whom he
stole four millions in counterfeit bonds! And
what a vast amount of time and patience and
cunning I expended to achieve that result!
It was the first time in my life that I was
played for a fool, and I frankly confess that I
was fooled that time to the queen's taste!''

Chapter VIII

THE BLACK PEARL

A VIOLENT ringing of the bell awakened the concierge of number nine, avenue Hoche. She pulled the door-string, grumbling:

"I thought everybody was in. It must be three o'clock!"

"Perhaps it is some one for the doctor," muttered her husband.

At that moment, a voice inquired:

"Doctor Harel . . . . what floor?"

"Third floor, left. But the doctor won't go out at night."

"He must go to-night."

The visitor entered the vestibule, ascended to the first floor, the second, the third, and, without stopping at the doctor's door, he continued to the fifth floor. There, he tried two keys. One of them fitted the lock.

"Ah! good!" he murmured, "that simplifies the business wonderfully. But before I commence work I had better arrange for my retreat. Let me see . . . . have I had sufficient time to rouse the doctor and be dismissed by him? Not yet . . . . a few minutes more.''

At the end of ten minutes, he descended the stairs, grumbling noisily about the doctor. The concierge opened the door for him and heard it click behind him. But the door did not lock, as the man had quickly inserted a piece of iron in the lock in such a manner that the bolt could not enter. Then, quietly, he entered the house again, unknown to the concierge. In case of alarm, his retreat was assured. Noiselessly, he ascended to the fifth floor once more. In the antechamber, by the light of his electric lantern, he placed his hat and overcoat on one of the chairs, took a seat on another, and covered his heavy shoes with felt slippers.

''Ouf! here I am—and how simple it was! I wonder why more people do not adopt the profitable and pleasant occupation of burglar. With a little care and reflection, it becomes a most delightful profession. Not too quiet and monotonous, of course, as it would then become wearisome.''

He unfolded a detailed plan of the apartment.

''Let me commence by locating myself.

Here, I see the vestibule in which I am sitting. On the street front, the drawing-room,
the boudoir and dining-room. Useless to
waste any time there, as it appears that the
countess has a deplorable taste . . . . not a
bibelot of any value! . . . Now, let's get down
to business! . . . Ah! here is a corridor; it
must lead to the bed chambers. At a distance
of three metres, I should come to the door of
the wardrobe-closet which connects with the
chamber of the countess." He folded his
plan, extinguished his lantern, and proceeded
down the corridor, counting his distance,
thus:

"One metre . . . . two metres . . . . three
metres. . . . Here is the door. . . . Mon Dieu,
how easy it is! Only a small, simple bolt now
separates me from the chamber, and I know
that the bolt is located exactly one metre,
forty-three centimetres, from the floor. So
that, thanks to a small incision I am about to
make, I can soon get rid of the bolt."

He drew from his pocket the necessary in-
struments. Then the following idea occurred
to him:

"Suppose, by chance, the door is not
bolted. I will try it first."

He turned the knob, and the door opened.

"My brave Lupin, surely fortune favors you. . . . What's to be done now? You know the situation of the rooms; you know the place in which the countess hides the black pearl. Therefore, in order to secure the black pearl, you have simply to be more silent than silence, more invisible than darkness itself."

Arsène Lupin was employed fully a half-hour in opening the second door—a glass door that led to the countess' bedchamber. But he accomplished it with so much skill and precaution, that even had the countess been awake, she would not have heard the slightest sound. According to the plan of the rooms that he holds, he has merely to pass around a reclining chair, which will bring him to an arm chair and, beyond that, a small table close to the bed. On the table, there was a box of letter-paper, and the black pearl was concealed in that box. He stooped and crept cautiously over the carpet, following the outlines of the reclining-chair. When he reached the extremity of it, he stopped in order to re-press the throbbing of his heart. Although he was not moved by any sense of fear, he found it impossible to overcome the nervous anxiety that one usually feels in the midst of profound silence. That circumstance astonished him, because he had passed through many more solemn moments without the slightest trace of emotion. No danger threatened him. Then why did his heart throb like an alarm-bell? Was it that sleeping woman who affected him? Was it the proximity of another pulsating heart?

He listened, and thought he could discern the rhythmical breathing of a person asleep. It gave him confidence, like the presence of a friend. He sought and found the armchair; then, by slow, cautious movements, advanced toward the table, feeling ahead of him with outstretched arm. His right hand touched one of the feet of the table. Ah! now, he had simply to rise, take the pearl, and escape. That was fortunate, as his heart was leaping in his breast like a wild beast, and made so much noise that he feared it would waken the countess. By a powerful effort of the will, he subdued the wild throbbing of his heart, and was about to rise from the floor when his left hand encountered, lying on the floor, an object which he recognized as a candlestick—an overturned candlestick. A moment later, his hand encountered another object: a clock—

one of those small travelling clocks, covered
with leather.

Well! What had happened? He could not
understand. That candlestick, that clock;
why were those articles not in their accustomed places? Ah! what had happened in
the dread silence of the night?

Suddenly a cry escaped him. He had
touched—oh! some strange, unutterable
thing! "No! no!" he thought, "it cannot
be. It is some fantasy of my excited brain."
For twenty seconds, thirty seconds, he remained motionless, terrified, his forehead
bathed with perspiration, and his fingers still
retained the sensation of that dreadful
contact.

Making a desperate effort, he ventured to
extend his arm again. Once more, his hand
encountered that strange, unutterable thing.
He felt it. He must feel it and find out what
it is. He found that it was hair, human hair,
and a human face; and that face was cold,
almost icy.

However frightful the circumstances may
be, a man like Arsène Lupin controls himself
and commands the situation as soon as he

learns what it is. So, Arsène Lupin quickly
brought his lantern into use. A woman was
lying before him, covered with blood. Her
neck and shoulders were covered with gaping
wounds. He leaned over her and made a
closer examination. She was dead.

"Dead! Dead!" he repeated, with a bewildered air.

He stared at those fixed eyes, that grim
mouth, that livid flesh, and that blood—all
that blood which had flowed over the carpet
and congealed there in thick, black spots. He
arose and turned on the electric lights. Then
he beheld all the marks of a desperate struggle. The bed was in a state of great disorder.
On the floor, the candlestick, and the clock
with the hands pointing to twenty minutes
after eleven; then, further away, an overturned chair; and, everywhere, there was
blood, spots of blood and pools of blood.

"And the black pearl?" he murmured.

The box of letter-paper was in its place.
He opened it, eagerly. The jewel-case was
there, but it was empty.

"Fichtre!" he muttered. "You boasted of
your good fortune much too soon, my friend
Lupin. With the countess lying cold and
dead, and the black pearl vanished, the sit-

uation is anything but pleasant. Get out of
here as soon as you can, or you may get into
serious trouble.''

Yet, he did not move.

''Get out of here? Yes, of course. Any
person would, except Arsène Lupin. He has
something better to do. Now, to proceed in
an orderly way. At all events, you have a
clear conscience. Let us suppose that you
are the commissary of police and that you are
proceeding to make an inquiry concerning
this affair—— Yes, but in order to do that,
I require a clearer brain. Mine is muddled
like a ragout.''

He tumbled into an armchair, with his
clenched hands pressed against his burning
forehead.

*　　　*　　　*　　　*　　　*

The murder of the avenue Hoche is one of
those which have recently surprised and puzzled the Parisian public, and, certainly, I
should never have mentioned the affair if the
veil of mystery had not been removed by
Arsène Lupin himself. No one else knew the
exact truth of the case.

Who did not know—from having met her
in the Bois—the fair Léontine Zalti, the once-
famous cantatrice, wife and widow of the

Count d'Andillot; the Zalti, whose luxury
dazzled all Paris some twenty years ago; the
Zalti who acquired an European reputation
for the magnificence of her diamonds and
pearls? It was said that she wore upon her
shoulders the capital of several banking-
houses and the gold mines of numerous Aus-
tralian companies. Skilful jewellers worked
for Zelti as they had formerly wrought for
kings and queens.

And who does not remember the catas-
trophe in which all that wealth was swallowed
up? Of all that marvellous collection, nothing remained except the famous black pearl.
The black pearl! That is to say a fortune, if
she had wished to part with it.

But she preferred to keep it, to live in a
commonplace apartment with her companion,
her cook, and a man-servant, rather than sell
that inestimable jewel. There was a reason
for it; a reason she was not afraid to dis-
close: the black pearl was the gift of an emperor! Almost ruined, and reduced to the
most mediocre existence, she remained faithful to the companion of her happy and brilliant youth. The black pearl never left her
possession. She wore it during the day, and,

at night, concealed it in a place known to her alone.

All these facts, being republished in the columns of the public press, served to stimulate curiosity; and, strange to say, but quite obvious to those who have the key to the mystery, the arrest of the presumed assassin only complicated the question and prolonged the excitement. Two days later, the newspapers published the following item:

"Information has reached us of the arrest of Victor Danègre, the servant of the Countess d'Andillot. The evidence against him is clear and convincing. On the silken sleeve of his liveried waistcoat, which chief detective Dudouis found in his garret between the mattresses of his bed, several spots of blood were discovered. In addition, a cloth-covered button was missing from that garment, and this button was found beneath the bed of the victim. ·

"It is supposed that, after dinner, in place of going to his own room, Danègre slipped into the wardrobe-closet, and, through the glass door, had seen the countess hide the precious black pearl. This is simply a theory, as yet unverified by any evidence. There is, also, another obscure point. At seven o'clock in the morning, Danègre went to the tobacco-shop on the Boulevard de Courcelles; the concierge and the shop-keeper both affirm this fact. On the other hand, the countess' companion and cook, who sleep at the end of the hall, both declare that, when they arose at eight o'clock, the door of the antechamber and the door of the kitchen were locked. These two persons have been in the service of the countess for twenty years, and are above suspicion. The question is: How did Danègre leave the apartment? Did he have another key? These are matters that the police will investigate."

As a matter of fact, the police investigation threw no light on the mystery. It was learned that Victor Danègre was a dangerous criminal, a drunkard and a debauchee. But, as they proceeded with the investigation, the mystery deepened and new complications arosé. In the first place, a young woman, Mlle. de Sinclèves, the cousin and sole heiress of the countess, declared that the countess, a month before her death, had written a letter to her and in it described the manner in which the black pearl was concealed. The letter disappeared on the day after she received it. Who had stolen it?

Again, the concierge related how she had
opened the door for a person who had inquired for Doctor Harel. On being questioned, the doctor testified that no one had
rung his bell. Then who was that person?
An accomplice?

The theory of an accomplice was thereupon
adopted by the press and public, and also by
Ganimard, the famous detective.

"Lupin is at the bottom of this affair," he
said to the judge.

"Bah!" exclaimed the judge, "you have
Lupin on the brain. You see him everywhere."

"I see him everywhere, because he is everywhere."

"Say rather that you see him every time
you encounter something you cannot explain.
Besides, you overlook the fact that the crime
was committed at twenty minutes past eleven
in the evening, as is shown by the clerk, while
the nocturnal visit, mentioned by the concierge, occurred at three o'clock in the
morning."

Officers of the law frequently form a hasty
conviction as to the guilt of a suspected person, and then distort all subsequent discov-
eries to conform to their established theory.

The deplorable antecedents of Victor Danègre, habitual criminal, drunkard and rake, in-
fluenced the judge, and despite the fact that
nothing new was discovered in corroboration
of the early clues, his official opinion remained firm and unshaken. He closed his
investigation, and, a few weeks later, the trial
commenced. It proved to be slow and tedious.
The judge was listless, and the public prose-
cutor presented the case in a careless manner. Under those circumstances, Danègre's
counsel had an easy task. He pointed out the
defects and inconsistencies of the case for the
prosecution, and argued that the evidence was
quite insufficient to convict the accused. Who
had made the key, the indispensable key without which Danègre, on leaving the apartment,
could not have locked the door behind him?
Who had ever seen such a key, and what had
become of it? Who had seen the assassin's
knife, and where is it now?

"In any event," argued the prisoner's
counsel, "the prosecution must prove, beyond
any reasonable doubt, that the prisoner committed the murder. The prosecution must
show that the mysterious individual who entered the house at three o'clock in the morning is not the guilty party. To be sure, the

clock indicated eleven o'clock. But what of
that? I contend, that proves nothing. The
assassin could turn the hands of the clock
to any hour he pleased, and thus deceive us
in regard to the exact hour of the crime.''

Victor Danègre was acquitted.

He left the prison on Friday about dusk in
the evening, weak and depressed by his six
months' imprisonment. The inquisition, the
solitude, the trial, the deliberations of the
jury, combined to fill him with a nervous fear.
At night, he had been afflicted with terrible
nightmares and haunted by weird visions of
the scaffold. He was a mental and physical
wreck.

Under the assumed name of Anatole Dufour, he rented a small room on the heights of
Montmartre, and lived by doing odd jobs
wherever he could find them. He led a pitiful
existence. Three times, he obtained regular
employment, only to be recognized and then
discharged. Sometimes, he had an idea that
men were following him—detectives, no
doubt, who were seeking to trap and denounce
him. He could almost feel the strong hand
of the law clutching him by the collar.

One evening, as he was eating his dinner
at a neighboring restaurant, a man entered

and took a seat at the same table. He was a person about forty years of age, and wore a frock-coat of doubtful cleanliness. He ordered soup, vegetables, and a bottle of wine. After he had finished his soup, he turned his eyes on Danègre, and gazed at him intently. Danègre winced. He was certain that this was one of the men who had been following him for several weeks. What did he want? Danègre tried to rise, but failed. His limbs refused to support him. The man poured himself a glass of wine, and then filled Danègre's glass. The man raised his glass, and said:

"To your health, Victor Danègre."

Victor started in alarm, and stammered:

"I! . . . . I! . . . . no, no . . . . I swear to you. . . ."

"You will swear what? That you are not yourself? The servant of the countess?"

"What servant? My name is Dufour. Ask the proprietor."

"Yes, Anatole Dufour to the proprietor of this restaurant, but Victor Danègre to the officers of the law."

"That's not true! Some one has lied to you."

The new-comer took a card from his pocket

and handed it to Victor, who read on it:
"Grimaudan, ex-inspector of the detective
force. Private business transacted." Victor
shuddered as he said:

"You are connected with the police?"

"No, not now, but I have a liking for the
business and I continue to work at it in a
manner more—profitable. From time to
time I strike upon a golden opportunity—
such as your case presents."

"My case?"

"Yes, yours. I assure you it is a most
promising affair, provided you are inclined to
be reasonable."

"But if I am not reasonable?"

"Oh! my good fellow, you are not in a
position to refuse me anything I may ask."

"What is it . . . . you want?" stammered
Victor, fearfully.

"Well, I will inform you in a few words.
I am sent by Mademoiselle de Sinclèves, the
heiress of the Countess d'Andillot."

"What for?"

"To recover the black pearl."

"Black pearl?"

"That you stole."

"But I haven't got it."

"You have it."

"If I had, then I would be the assassin."

"You are the assassin."

Danègre showed a forced smile.

"Fortunately for me, monsieur, the Assize-court was not of your opinion. The jury returned an unanimous verdict of acquittal. And when a man has a clear conscience and twelve good men in his favor——"

The ex-inspector seized him by the arm, and said:

"No fine phrases, my boy. Now, listen to me and weigh my words carefully. You will find they are worthy of your consideration. Now, Danègre, three weeks before the murder, you abstracted the cook's key to the servants' door, and had a duplicate key made by a locksmith named Outard, 244 rue Ober-kampf."

"It's a lie—it's a lie!" growled Victor. "No person has seen that key. There is no such key."

"Here it is."

After a silence, Grimaudan continued:

"You killed the countess with a knife purchased by you at the Bazar de la Republique on the same day as you ordered the duplicate key. It has a triangular blade with a groove running from end to end."

"That is all nonsense. You are simply guessing at something you don't know. No one ever saw the knife."

"Here it is."

Victor Danègre recoiled. The ex-inspector continued:

"There are some spots of rust upon it. Shall I tell you how they came there?"

"Well! . . . . you have a key and a knife. Who can prove that they belong to me?"

"The locksmith, and the clerk from whom you bought the knife. I have already refreshed their memories, and, when you confront them, they cannot fail to recognize you."

His speech was dry and hard, with a tone of firmness and precision. Danègre was trembling with fear, and yet he struggled desperately to maintain an air of indifference.

"Is that all the evidence you have?"

"Oh! no, not at all. I have plenty more. For instance, after the crime, you went out the same way as you had entered. But, in the centre of the wardrobe-room, being seized by some sudden fear, you leaned against the wall for support."

"How do you know that? No one could

know such a thing,'' argued the desperate man.

"The police know nothing about it, of course. They never think of lighting a candle and examining the walls. But if they had done so, they would have found on the white plaster a faint red spot, quite distinct enough, however, to trace in it the imprint of your thumb which you had pressed against the wall while it was wet with blood. Now, as you are well aware, under the Bertillon system, thumb-marks are one of the principal means of identification.''

Victor Danègre was livid; great drops of perspiration rolled down his face and fell upon the table. He gazed, with a wild look, at the strange man who had narrated' the story of his crime as faithfully as if he had been an invisible witness to it. Overcome and powerless, Victor bowed his head. He felt that it was useless to struggle against this marvellous man. So he said:

"How much will you give me, if I give you the pearl?''

"Nothing.''

"Oh! you are joking! Or do you mean that I should give you an article worth thousands

and hundreds of thousands and get nothing in
return?"

"You will get your life. Is that nothing?"

The unfortunate man shuddered. Then
Grimaudan added, in a milder tone:

"Come, Danègre, that pearl has no value in
your hands. It is quite impossible for you to
sell it; so what is the use of your keeping it?"

"There are pawnbrokers . . . . and, some
day, I will be able to get something for it."

"But that day may be too late."

"Why?"

"Because by that time you may be in the
hands of the police, and, with the evidence
that I can furnish—the knife, the key, the
thumb-mark—what will become of you?"

Victor rested his head on his hands and reflected. He felt that he was lost, irremedia-
bly lost, and, at the same time, a sense of
weariness and depression overcame him. He
murmured, faintly:

"When must I give it to you?"

"To-night—within an hour."

"If I refuse?"

"If you refuse, I shall post this letter to
the Procureur of the Republic; in which letter Mademoiselle de Sinclèves denounces you
as the assassin."

Danègre poured out two glasses of wine which he drank in rapid succession, then, rising, said:

"Pay the bill, and let us go. I have had enough of the cursed affair."

Night had fallen. The two men walked down the rue Lepic and followed the exterior boulevards in the direction of the Place de l'Etoile. They pursued their way in silence; Victor had a stooping carriage and a dejected face. When they reached the Parc Monceau, he said:

"We are near the house."

"Parbleu! You only left the house once, before your arrest, and that was to go to the tobacco-shop."

"Here it is," said Danègre, in a dull voice.

They passed along the garden wall of the countess' house, and crossed a street on a corner of which stood the tobacco-shop. A few steps farther on, Danègre stopped; his limbs shook beneath him, and he sank to a bench.

"Well! what now?" demanded his companion.

"It is there."

"Where? Come, now, no nonsense!"

"There—in front of us."

"Where?"

"Between two paving-stones."

"Which?"

"Look for it."

"Which stones?"

Victor made no reply.

"Ah; I see!" exclaimed Grimaudan, "you want me to pay for the information."

"No . . . . but . . . . I am afraid I will starve to death."

"So! that is why you hesitate. Well, I'll not be hard on you. How much do you want?"

"Enough to buy a steerage passage to America."

"All right."

"And a hundred francs to keep me until I get work there."

"You shall have two hundred. Now, speak."

"Count the paving-stones to the right from the sewer-hole. The pearl is between the twelfth and thirteenth."

"In the gutter?"

"Yes, close to the sidewalk."

Grimaudan glanced around to see if any-one were looking. Some tram-cars and pe-destrians were passing. But, bah! they will not suspect anything. He opened his pocket-knife and thrust it between the twelfth and thirteenth stones.

"And if it is not there?" he said to Victor.

"It must be there, unless someone saw me stoop down and hide it."

Could it be possible that the black pearl had been cast into the mud and filth of the gutter to be picked up by the first comer? The black pearl—a fortune!

"How far is it down?" he asked.

"About ten centimetres."

He dug up the wet earth. The point of his knife struck something. He enlarged the hole with his finger. Then he abstracted the black pearl from its filthy hiding-place.

"Good! Here are your two hundred francs. I will send you the ticket for America."

On the following day, this article was published in the *Echo de France*, and was copied by the leading papers throughout the world:

"Yesterday, the famous black pearl came into the possession of Arsène Lupin, who recovered it from the murderer of the Countess d'Andillot. In a short time, fac-similes of that precious jewel will be exhibited in London, St. Petersburg, Calcutta, Buenos Ayres and New York.

"Arsène Lupin will be pleased to consider
all propositions submitted to him through his
agents."

*   *   *   *   *

"And that is how crime is always punished
and virtue rewarded," said Arsène Lupin,
after he had told me the foregoing history of
the black pearl.

"And that is how you, under the assumed
name of Grimaudan, ex-inspector of detectives, were chosen by fate to deprive the criminal of the benefit of his crime."

"Exactly. And I confess that the affair
gives me infinite satisfaction and pride. The
forty minutes that I passed in the apartment
of the Countess d'Andillot, after learning of
her death, were the most thrilling and absorb-
ing moments of my life. In those forty minutes, involved as I was in a most dangerous
plight, I calmly studied the scene of the murder and reached the conclusion that the crime
must have been committed by one of the house
servants. I also decided that, in order to get
the pearl, that servant must be arrested, and
so I left the waistcoat button; it was necessary, also, for me to hold some convincing
evidence of his guilt, so I carried away the

knife which I found upon the floor, and the key which I found in the lock. I closed and locked the door, and erased the finger-marks from the plaster in the wardrobe-closet. In my opinion, that was one of those flashes—"

"Of genius," I said, interrupting.

"Of genius, if you wish. But, I flatter myself, it would not have occurred to the average mortal. To frame, instantly, the two elements of the problem—an arrest and an acquittal; to make use of the formidable machinery of the law to crush and humble my victim, and reduce him to a condition in which, when free, he would be certain to fall into the trap I was laying for him!"

"Poor devil—"

"Poor devil, do you say? Victor Danègre, the assassin! He might have descended to the lowest depths of vice and crime, if he had retained the black pearl. Now, he lives! Think of that: Victor Danègre is alive!

"And you have the black pearl."

He took it out of one of the secret pockets of his wallet, examined it, gazed at it tenderly, and caressed it with loving fingers, and sighed, as he said:

"What cold Russian prince, what vain and

foolish rajah may some day possess this
priceless treasure! Or, perhaps, some American millionaire is destined to become the
owner of this morsel of exquisite beauty that
once adorned the fair bosom of Leontine
Zalti, the Countess d'Andillot.''

CHAPTER IX

SHERLOCK HOLMES ARRIVES TOO LATE

"IT is really remarkable, Velmont, what a close resemblance you bear to Arsène Lupin!"

"How do you know?"

"Oh! like everyone else, from photographs, no two of which are alike, but each of them leaves the impression of a face....something like yours."

Horace Velmont displayed some vexation.

"Quite so, my dear Devanne. And, believe me, you are not the first one who has noticed it."

"It is so striking," persisted Devanne, "that if you had not been recommended to me by my cousin d'Estevan, and if you were not the celebrated artist whose beautiful marine views I so admire, I have no doubt I should have warned the police of your presence in Dieppe."

This sally was greeted with an outburst of laughter. The large dining-hall of the Château de Thibermesnil contained on this

occasion, besides Velmont, the following
guests: Father Gélis, the parish priest, and
a dozen officers whose regiments were quar-
tered in the vicinity and who had accepted
the invitation of the banker Georges Devanne
and his mother. One of the officers then remarked:

"I understand that an exact description
of Arsène Lupin has been furnished to all
the police along this coast since his daring
exploit on the Paris-Havre express."

"I suppose so," said Devanne. "That was
three months ago; and a week later, I made
the acquaintance of our friend Velmont at
the casino, and, since then, he has honored
me with several visits—an agreeable pream-
ble to a more serious visit that he will pay
me one of these days—or, rather, one of these
nights."

This speech evoked another round of laughter, and the guests then passed into the ancient "Hall of the Guards," a vast room with
a high ceiling, which occupied the entire
lower part of the Tour Guillaume—William's
Tower—and wherein Georges Devanne had
collected the incomparable treasures which
the lords of Thibermesnil had accumulated
through many centuries. It contained an-

cient chests, credences, andirons and chandeliers. The stone walls were overhung with magnificent tapestries. The deep embrasures of the four windows were furnished with benches, and the Gothic windows were composed of small panes of colored glass set in a leaden frame. Between the door and the window to the left stood an immense bookcase of Renaissance style, on the pediment of which, in letters of gold, was the word "Thibermesnil," and, below it, the proud family device: "Fais ce que veulx" (Do what thou wishest). When the guests had lighted their cigars, Devanne resumed the conversation.

"And remember, Velmont, you have no time to lose; in fact, to-night is the last chance you will have."

"How so?" asked the painter, who appeared to regard the affair as a joke. Devanne was about to reply, when his mother motioned to him to keep silent, but the excitement of the occasion and a desire to interest his guests urged him to speak.

"Bah!" he murmured. "I can tell it now. It won't do any harm."

The guests drew closer, and he commenced

to speak with the satisfied air of a man who has an important announcement to make.

"To-morrow afternoon at four o'clock, Sherlock Holmes, the famous English detective, for whom such a thing as mystery does not exist; Sherlock Holmes, the most remarkable solver of enigmas the world has ever known, that marvelous man who would seem to be the creation of a romantic novelist —Sherlock Holmes will be my guest!"

Immediately, Devanne was the target of numerous eager questions. "Is Sherlock Holmes really coming?" "Is it so serious as that?" "Is Arsène Lupin really in this neighborhood?"

"Arsène Lupin and his band are not far away. Besides the robbery of the Baron Cahorn, he is credited with the thefts at Montigny, Gruchet and Crasville. And now it is my turn."

"Has he sent you a warning, as he did to Baron Cahorn?"

"No," replied Devanne, "he can't work the same trick twice."

"What then?"

"I will show you."

He rose, and pointing to a small empty

space between two enormous folios on one of
the shelves of the bookcase, he said:

"There used to be a book there—a book
of the sixteenth century entitled 'Chronique
de Thibermesnil,' which contained the history
of the castle since its construction by Duke
Rollo on the site of a former feudal fortress.
There were three engraved plates in the
book; one of which was a general view of the
whole estate; another, the plan of the build-
ings; and the third—I call your attention to
it, particularly—the third was the sketch of
a subterranean passage, one entrance to
which is outside the first line of ramparts,
while the other end of the passage is here,
in this very room. Well, that book disappeared a month ago."

"The deuce!" said Velmont, "that looks
bad. But it doesn't seem to be a sufficient
reason for sending for Sherlock Holmes."

"Certainly, that was not sufficient in itself,
but another incident happened that gives the
disappearance of the book a special signifi-
cance. There was another copy of this book
in the National Library at Paris, and the two
books differed in certain details relating to
the subterranean passage; for instance, each
of them contained drawings and annotations,

not printed, but written in ink and more or
less effaced. I knew those facts, and I knew
that the exact location of the passage could
be determined only by a comparison of the
two books. Now, the day after my book disappeared, the book was called for in the National Library by a reader who carried it
away, and no one knows how the theft was
effected.''

The guests uttered many exclamations of
surprise.

''Certainly, the affair looks serious,'' said
one.

''Well, the police investigated the matter,
and, as usual, discovered no clue whatever.''

''They never do, when Arsène Lupin is
concerned in it.''

''Exactly; and so I decided to ask the assistance of Sherlock Holmes, who replied that
he was ready and anxious to enter the lists
with Arsène Lupin.

''What glory for Arsène Lupin!'' said Velmont. ''But if our national thief, as they call
him, has no evil designs on your castle, Sherlock Holmes will have his trip in vain.''

''There are other things that will interest
him, such as the discovery of the subterranean passage.''

"But you told us that one end of the passage was outside the ramparts and the other end was in this very room!"

"Yes, but in what part of the room? The line which represents the passage on the charts ends here with a small circle marked with the letters 'T. G.,' which no doubt stand for 'Tour Guillaume.' But the tower is round, and who can tell the exact spot at which the passage touches the tower?"

Devanne lighted a second cigar and poured himself a glass of benedictine. His guests pressed him with questions and he was pleased to observe the interest that his remarks had created. Then he continued:

"The secret is lost. No one knows it. The legend is to the effect that the former lords of the castle transmitted the secret from father to son on their deathbeds, until Geoffroy, the last of the race, was beheaded during the Revolution in his nineteenth year."

"That is over a century ago. Surely, someone has looked for it since that time?"

"Yes, but they failed to find it. After I purchased the castle, I made a diligent search for it, but without success. You must remember that this tower is surrounded by water and connected with the castle only by a bridge; consequently, the passage must be underneath the old moat. The plan that was in the book in the National Library showed a series of stairs with a total of forty-eight steps, which indicates a depth of more than ten meters. And the scale annexed to the other plan gives the distance as two hundred meters. You see, the mystery lies within the walls of this room, and yet I dislike to tear them down.''

"Is there nothing to show where it is?''

"Nothing.''

"Mon. Devanne, we should turn our attention to the two quotations," suggested Father Gélis.

"Oh!'' exclaimed Mon. Devanne, laughing, "our worthy father is fond of reading memoirs and delving into the musty archives of the castle. Everything relating to Thibermesnil interests him greatly. But the quotations that he mentions only serve to complicate the mystery. He has read somewhere that two kings of France have known the key to the puzzle.''

"Two kings of France! Who were they?''

"Henry the Fourth and Louis the Sixteenth. And the legend runs like this: On the eve of the battle of Arques, Henry the

Fourth spent the night in this castle. At eleven o'clock in the evening, Louise de Tancarville, the prettiest woman in Normandy, was brought into the castle through the subterranean passage by Duke Edgard, who, at the same time, informed the king of the secret passage. Afterward, the king confided the secret to his minister Sully, who, in turn, relates the story in his book, ''Royales Economies d'Etat,'' without making any comment upon it, but linking with it this incomprehensible sentence: 'Turn one eye on the bee that shakes, the other eye will lead to God!'

After a brief silence, Velmont laughed and said:

''Certainly, it doesn't throw a dazzling light upon the subject.''

''No; but Father Gélis claims that Sully concealed the key to the mystery in this strange sentence in order to keep the secret from the secretaries to whom he dictated his memoirs.''

''That is an ingenious theory,'' said Velmont.

''Yes, and it may be nothing more; I cannot see that it throws any light on the mysterious riddle.''

''And was it also to receive the visit of a

lady that Louis the Sixteenth caused the
passage to be opened?''

''I don't know,'' said Mon. Devanne. All
I can say is that the king stopped here one
night in 1784, and that the famous Iron Casket found in the Louvre contained a paper
bearing these words in the king's own writing: 'Thibermesnil 3-4-11.''

Horace Velmont laughed heartily, and exclaimed:

''At last! And now that we have the magic
key, where is the man who can fit it to the
invisible lock?''

''Laugh as much as you please, monsieur,''
said Father Gèlis, ''but I am confident the
solution is contained in those two sentences,
and some day we will find a man able to in-
terpret them.''

''Sherlock Holmes is the man,'' said Mon.
Devanne, ''unless Arsène Lupin gets ahead
of him. What is your opinion, Velmont?''

Velmont arose, placed his hand on Devanne's shoulder, and declared:

''I think that the information furnished by
your book and the book of the National Library was deficient in a very important detail
which you have now supplied. I thank you
for it.''

"What is it?"

"The missing key. Now that I have it, I can go to work at once," said Velmont.

"Of course; without losing a minute," said Devanne, smiling.

"Not even a second!" replied Velmont. "To-night, before the arrival of Sherlock Holmes, I must plunder your castle."

"You have no time to lose. Oh! by the way, I can drive you over this evening."

"To Dieppe?"

"Yes. I am going to meet Monsieur and Madame d'Androl and a young lady of their acquaintance who are to arrive by the midnight train."

Then addressing the officers, Devanne added:

"Gentlemen, I shall expect to see all of you at breakfast to-morrow."

The invitation was accepted. The company dispersed, and a few moments later Devanne and Velmont were speeding toward Dieppe in an automobile. Devanne dropped the artist in front of the Casino, and proceeded to the railway station. At twelve o'clock his friends alighted from the train. A half hour later the automobile was at the entrance to the castle. At one o'clock, after a light supper,

they retired.   The lights were extinguished,
and the castle was enveloped in the darkness
and silence of the night.

     *   *   *   *   *

The moon appeared through a rift in the
clouds, and filled the drawing-room with its
bright white light.   But only for a moment.
Then the moon again retired behind its
ethereal draperies, and darkness and silence
reigned supreme.   No sound could be heard,
save the monotonous ticking of the clock.   It
struck two, and then continued its endless
repetitions of the seconds.   Then, three
o'clock.

Suddenly, something clicked, like the opening and closing of a signal-disc that warns
the passing train.   A thin stream of light
flashed to every corner of the room, like an
arrow that leaves behind it a trail of light.
It shot forth from the central fluting of a col-
umn that supported the pediment of the
bookcase.   It rested for a moment on the
panel opposite like a glittering circle of bur-
nished silver, then flashed in all directions
like a guilty eye that scrutinizes every
shadow.   It disappeared for a short time,
but burst forth again as a whole section of

the bookcase revolved on a pivot and disclosed a large opening like a vault.

A man entered, carrying an electric lantern. He was followed by a second man and a third, who carried a coil of rope and various tools. The leader inspected the room, listened a moment, and said:

"Call the others."

Then eight men, stout fellows with resolute faces, entered the room, and immediately commenced to remove the furnishings. Arsène Lupin passed quickly from one piece of furniture to another, examined each, and, according to its size or artistic value, he directed his men to take it or leave it. If ordered to be taken, it was carried to the gaping mouth of the tunnel, and ruthlessly thrust into the bowels of the earth. Such was the fate of six armchairs, six small Louis XV chairs, a quantity of Aubusson tapestries, some candelabra, paintings by Fragonard and Nattier, a bust by Houdon, and some statuettes. Sometimes, Lupin would linger before a beautiful chest or a superb picture, and sigh:

"That is too heavy....too large....what a pity!"

In forty minutes the room was dismantled;

and it had been accomplished in such an orderly manner and with as little noise as if the various articles had been packed and wadded for the occasion.

Lupin said to the last man who departed by way of the tunnel:

"You need not come back. You understand, that as soon as the auto-van is loaded, you are to proceed to the grange at Roquefort."

"But you, patron?"

"Leave me the motor-cycle."

When the man had disappeared, Arsène Lupin pushed the section of the bookcase back into its place, carefully effaced the traces of the men's footsteps, raised a portière, and entered a gallery, which was the only means of communication between the tower and the castle. In the center of this gallery there was a glass cabinet which had attracted Lupin's attention. It contained a valuable collection of watches, snuff-boxes, rings, chatelaines and miniatures of rare and beautiful workmanship. He forced the lock with a small jimmy, and experienced a great pleasure in handling those gold and silver ornaments, those exquisite and delicate works of art.

He carried a large linen bag, specially prepared for the removal of such knick-knacks. He filled it. Then he filled the pockets of his coat, waistcoat and trousers. And he was just placing over his left arm a number of pearl reticules when he heard a slight sound. He listened. No, he was not deceived. The noise continued. Then he remembered that, at one end of the gallery, there was a stairway leading to an unoccupied apartment, but which was probably occupied that night by the young lady whom Mon. Devanne had brought from Dieppe with his other visitors.

Immediately he extinguished his lantern, and had scarcely gained the friendly shelter of a window-embrasure, when the door at the top of the stairway was opened and a feeble light illumined the gallery. He could feel— for, concealed by a curtain, he could not see— that a woman was cautiously descending the upper steps of the stairs. He hoped she would come no closer. Yet, she continued to descend, and even advanced some distance into the room. Then she uttered a faint cry. No doubt she had discovered the broken and dismantled cabinet.

She advanced again. Now he could smell the perfume, and hear the throbbing of her heart as she drew closer to the window where he was concealed. She passed so close that her skirt brushed against the window-curtain, and Lupin felt that she suspected the presence of another, behind her, in the shadow, within reach of her hand. He thought: "She is afraid. She will go away." But she did not go. The candle, that she carried in her trembling hand, grew brighter. She turned, hesitated a moment, appeared to listen, then suddenly drew aside the curtain.

They stood face to face. Arsène was astounded. He murmured, involuntarily:

"You—you—mademoiselle."

It was Miss Nelly. Miss Nelly! his fellow-passenger on the transatlantic steamer, who had been the subject of his dreams on that memorable voyage, who had been a witness to his arrest, and who, rather than betray him, had dropped into the water the kodak in which he had concealed the bank-notes and diamonds. Miss Nelly! that charming creature, the memory of whose face has sometimes cheered, sometimes saddened the long hours of his imprisonment.

It was such an unexpected encounter that brought them face to face in that castle at that hour of the night, that they could not move, nor utter a word; they were amazed, hypnotized, each at the sudden apparition of the other. Trembling with emotion, Miss Nelly staggered to a seat. He remained standing in front of her.

Gradually, he realized the situation and conceived the impression he must have produced at that moment with his arms laden with knick-knacks, and his pockets and a linen sack overflowing with plunder. He was overcome with confusion, and he actually blushed to find himself in the position of a thief caught in the act. To her, henceforth, he was a thief, a man who puts his hand in another's pocket, who steals into houses and robs people while they sleep.

A watch fell upon the floor; then another. These were followed by other articles which slipped from his grasp one by one. Then, actuated by a sudden decision, he dropped the other articles into an armchair, emptied his pockets and unpacked his sack. He felt very uncomfortable in Nelly's presence, and stepped toward her with the intention of speaking to her, but she shuddered, rose quickly and fled toward the salon. The portière closed behind her. He followed her. She was standing trembling and amazed at the sight of the devastated room. He said to her, at once:

"To-morrow, at three o'clock, everything will be returned. The furniture will be brought back."

She made no reply, so he repeated:

"I promise it. To-morrow, at three o'clock. Nothing in the world could induce me to break that promise....To-morrow, at three o'clock."

Then followed a long silence that he dared not break, whilst the agitation of the young girl caused him a feeling of genuine regret. Quietly, without a word, he turned away, thinking: "I hope she will go away. I can't endure her presence." But the young girl suddenly spoke, and stammered:

"Listen .... footsteps .... I hear some-one...."

He looked at her with astonishment. She seemed to be overwhelmed by the thought of approaching peril.

"I don't hear anything," he said.

"But you must go—you must escape!"

"Why should I go?"

"Because—you must. Oh! do not remain here another minute. Go!"

She ran, quickly, to the door leading to the

gallery and listened. No, there was no one there. Perhaps the noise was outside. She waited a moment, then returned reassured.

But Arsène Lupin had disappeared.

*   *   *   *   *

As soon as Mon. Devanne was informed of the pillage of his castle, he said to himself: It was Velmont who did it, and Velmont is Arsène Lupin. That theory explained everything, and there was no other plausible explanation. And yet the idea seemed preposterous. It was ridiculous to suppose that Velmont was anyone else than Velmont, the famous artist, and club-fellow of his cousin d'Estevan. So, when the captain of the gendarmes arrived to investigate the affair, Devanne did not even think of mentioning his absurd theory.

Throughout the forenoon there was a lively commotion at the castle. The gendarmes, the local police, the chief of police from Dieppe, the villagers, all circulated to and fro in the halls, in the park, or about the walls of the castle, examining every nook and corner that was open to their inspection. The approach of the manoeuvring troops, the rattling fire of the musketry, added to the picturesque character of the scene.

The preliminary search furnished no clue. Neither the doors nor windows showed any signs of having been disturbed. Consequently, the removal of the goods must have been effected by means of the secret passage. Yet, there were no indications of footsteps on the floor, nor any unusual marks upon the walls.

Their investigation revealed, however, one curious fact that denoted the whimsical character of Arsène Lupin: the famous Chronique of the sixteenth century had been restored to its accustomed place in the library and, beside it, there was a similar book, which was none other than the volume stolen from the National Library.

At eleven o'clock the military officers arrived. Devanne welcomed them with his usual gayety; for, no matter how much chagrin he might suffer from the loss of his artistic treasures, his great wealth enabled him to bear his loss philosophically. His guests, Monsieur and Madame d'Androl and Miss Nelly, were introduced; and it was then noticed that one of the expected guests had not arrived. It was Horace Velmont. Would he come? His absence had awakened the sus-

picions of Mon. Devanne. But at twelve
o'clock he arrived. Devanne exclaimed:

"Ah! here you are!"

"Why, am I not punctual?" asked Velmont.

"Yes, and I am surprised that you are....
after such a busy night! I suppose you know
the news?"

"What news?"

"You have robbed the castle."

"Nonsense!" exclaimed Velmont, smiling.

"Exactly as I predicted. But, first escort
Miss Underdown to the dining-room. Mademoiselle, allow me—"

He stopped, as he remarked the extreme
agitation of the young girl. Then, recalling
the incident, he said:

"Ah! of course, you met Arsène Lupin on
the steamer, before his arrest, and you are
astonished at the resemblance. Is that it?"

She did not reply. Velmont stood before
her, smiling. He bowed. She took his proffered arm. He escorted her to her place, and
took his seat opposite her. During the breakfast, the conversation related exclusively to
Arsène Lupin, the stolen goods, the secret
passage, and Sherlock Holmes. It was only
at the close of the repast, when the conversa-

tion had drifted to other subjects, that Ve
mont took any part in it. Then he was, b
turns, amusing and grave, talkative and pe
sive. And all his remarks seemed to b
directed to the young girl. But she, qui
absorbed, did not appear to hear them.

Coffee was served on the terrace overloo
ing the court of honor and the flower garde
in front of the principal façade. The reg
mental band played on the lawn, and score
of soldiers and peasants wandered throug
the park.

Miss Nelly had not forgotten, for on
moment, Lupin's solemn promise: "To-mo
row, at three o'clock, everything will b
returned."

At three o'clock! And the hands of th
great clock in the right wing of the castle no
marked twenty minutes to three. In spite o
herself, her eyes wandered to the clock ever
minute. She also watched Velmont, who wa
calmly swinging to and fro in a comfortab.
rocking-chair.

Ten minutes to three!.... Five minute
to three!.... Nelly was impatient and anx
ious. Was it possible that Arsène Lupi
would carry out his promise at the appointe
hour, when the castle, the courtyard, and th

park were filled with people, and at the very moment when the officers of the law were pursuing their investigations? And yet.... Arsène Lupin had given her his solemn promise. "It will be exactly as he said," thought she, so deeply was she impressed with the authority, energy and assurance of that remarkable man. To her, it no longer assumed the form of a miracle, but, on the contrary, a natural incident that must occur in the ordinary course of events. Once, their eyes met. She blushed, and turned her head.

Three o'clock! The great clock struck slowly: one....two....three!.... Horace Velmont took out his watch, glanced at the clock, then returned the watch to his pocket. A few seconds passed in silence; and then the crowd in the courtyard parted to give passage to two wagons, that had just entered the park-gate, each drawn by two horses. They were army-wagons, such as are used for the transportation of provisions, tents, and other necessary military stores. They stopped in front of the main entrance, and a commissary-sergeant leaped from one of the wagons and enquired for Mon. Devanne. A moment later, that gentleman emerged from the house, descended the steps, and, under the

canvas covers of the wagons, beheld his furniture, pictures and ornaments carefully
packed and arranged.

When questioned, the sergeant produced
an order that he had received from the officer
of the day. By that order, the second company of the fourth battalion were commanded
to proceed to the crossroads of Halleux in
the forest of Arques, gather up the furniture
and other articles deposited there, and deliver
same to Monsieur Georges Devanne, owner
of the Thibermesnil castle, at three o'clock.
Signed: Col. Beauvel.

"At the crossroads," explained the sergeant, "we found everything ready, lying on
the grass, guarded by some passers-by. It
seemed very strange, but the order was
imperative."

One of the officers examined the signature.
He declared it a forgery; but a clever imita-
tion. Then the wagons were unloaded, and
the goods restored to their proper places in
the castle.

During this commotion, Nelly had remained
alone at the extreme end of the terrace, absorbed by confused and distracting thoughts.
Suddenly, she observed Velmont approaching
her. She would have avoided him, but the

balustrade that surrounded the terrace cut
off her retreat. She was cornered. She could
not move. A gleam of sunshine, passing
through the scant foliage of a bamboo, lighted
up her beautiful golden hair. Some one spoke
to her in a low voice:

"Have I not kept my promise?"

Arsène Lupin stood close to her. No one
else was near. He repeated, in a calm, soft
voice:

"Have I not kept my promise?"

He expected a word of thanks, or at least
some slight movement that would betray her
interest in the fulfilment of his promise. But
she remained silent.

Her scornful attitude annoyed Arsène
Lupin; and he realized the vast distance that
separated him from Miss Nelly, now that she
had learned the truth. He would gladly have
justified himself in her eyes, or at least
pleaded extenuating circumstances, but he
perceived the absurdity and futility of such
an attempt. Finally, dominated by a surging
flood of memories, he murmured:

"Ah! how long ago that was! You remember the long hours on the deck of the
Provence. Then, you carried a rose in your
hand, a white rose like the one you carry

to-day. I asked you for it. You pretended
you did not hear me. After you had gone
away, I found the rose—forgotten, no doubt
—and I kept it.''

She made no reply. She seemed to be far
away. He continued:

''In memory of those happy hours, forget
what you have learned since. Separate the
past from the present. Do not regard me
as the man you saw last night, but look at
me, if only for a moment, as you did in those
far-off days when I was Bernard d'Andrezy,
for a short time. Will you, please?''

She raised her eyes and looked at him as
he had requested. Then, without saying a
word, she pointed to a ring he was wearing
on his forefinger. Only the ring was visible;
but the setting, which was turned toward the
palm of his hand, consisted of a magnificent
ruby. Arsène Lupin blushed. The ring belonged to Georges Devanne. He smiled
bitterly, and said:

''You are right. Nothing can be changed.
Arsène Lupin is now and always will be
Arsène Lupin. To you, he cannot be even
so much as a memory. Pardon me.... I
should have known that any attention I may

now offer you is simply an insult. Forgive
me.''

He stepped aside, hat in hand. Nelly
passed before him. He was inclined to detain
her and beseech her forgiveness. But his
courage failed, and he contented himself by
following her with his eyes, as he had done
when she descended the gangway to the pier
at New York. She mounted the steps leading
to the door, and disappeared within the
house. He saw her no more.

A cloud obscured the sun. Arsène Lupin
stood watching the imprints of her tiny feet
in the sand. Suddenly, he gave a start. Upon
the box which contained the bamboo, beside
which Nelly had been standing, he saw the
rose, the white rose which he had desired
but dared not ask for. Forgotten, no doubt
—it, also! But how—designedly or through
distraction? He seized it eagerly. Some of
its petals fell to the ground. He picked them
up, one by one, like precious relics.
64—LUPIN—Mitchell.

"Come!" he said to himself, "I have
nothing more to do here. I must think of
my safety, before Sherlock Holmes arrives.''

    *   *   *   *   *

The park was deserted, but some gen-

darmes were stationed at the park-gate. He
entered a grove of pine trees, leaped over
the wall, and, as a short cut to the railroad
station, followed a path across the fields.
After walking about ten minutes, he arrived
at a spot where the road grew narrower and
ran between two steep banks. In this ravine,
he met a man travelling in the opposite direction. It was a man about fifty years of age,
tall, smooth-shaven, and wearing clothes of
a foreign cut. He carried a heavy cane, and
a small satchel was strapped across his
shoulder. When they met, the stranger
spoke, with a slight English accent:

"Excuse me, monsieur, is this the way to
the castle?"

"Yes, monsieur, straight ahead, and turn
to the left when you come to the wall. They
are expecting you."

"Ah!"

"Yes, my friend Devanne told us last night
that you were coming, and I am delighted to
be the first to welcome you. Sherlock Holmes
has no more ardent admirer than....my-
self."

There was a touch of irony in his voice
that he quickly regretted, for Sherlock
Holmes scrutinized him from head to foot

with such a keen, penetrating eye that Arsène Lupin experienced the sensation of being seized, imprisoned and registered by that look more thoroughly and precisely than he had ever been by a camera.

"My negative is taken now," he thought, "and it will be useless to use a disguise with that man. He would look right through it. But, I wonder, has he recognized me?"

They bowed to each other as if about to part. But, at that moment, they heard a sound of horses' feet, accompanied by a clinking of steel. It was the gendarmes. The two men were obliged to draw back against the embankment, amongst the bushes, to avoid the horses. The gendarmes passed by, but, as they followed each other at a considerable distance, they were several minutes in doing so. And Lupin was thinking:

"It all depends on that question: has he recognized me? If so, he will probably take advantage of the opportunity. It is a trying situation."

When the last horseman had passed, Sherlock Holmes stepped forth and brushed the dust from his clothes. Then, for a moment, he and Arsène Lupin gazed at each other; and, if a person could have seen them at that

moment, it would have been an interesting
sight, and memorable as the first meeting of
two remarkable men, so strange, so power-
fully equipped, both of superior quality, and
destined by fate, through their peculiar attri-
butes, to hurl themselves one at the other
like two equal forces that nature opposes,
one against the other, in the realms of space.

Then the Englishman said: "Thank you,
monsieur."

"You are quite welcome," replied Arsène
Lupin.

They parted. Lupin went toward the railway station, and Sherlock Holmes continued
on his way to the castle.

The local officers had given up the investigation after several hours of fruitless efforts,
and the people at the castle were awaiting
the arrival of the English detective with a
lively curiosity. At first sight, they were a
little disappointed on account of his commonplace appearance, which differed so greatly
from the pictures they had formed of him in
their own minds. He did not in any way
resemble the romantic hero, the mysterious
and diabolical personage that the name of
Sherlock Holmes had evoked in their imagi-

nations. However, Mon. Devanne exclaimed, with much gusto:

"Ah! monsieur, you are here! I am delighted to see you. It is a long-deferred pleasure. Really, I scarcely regret what has happened, since it affords me the opportunity to meet you. But, how did you come?"

"By the train."

"But I sent my automobile to meet you at the station."

"An official reception, eh? with music and fireworks! Oh! no, not for me. That is not the way I do business, grumbled the Englishman.

This speech disconcerted Devanne, who replied, with a forced smile:

"Fortunately, the business has been greatly simplified since I wrote to you."

"In what way?"

"The robbery took place last night."

"If you had not announced my intended visit, it is probable the robbery would not have been committed last night."

"When, then?"

"To-morrow, or some other day."

"And in that case?"

"Lupin would have been trapped," said the detective.

"And my furniture?"

"Would not have been carried away."

"Ah! but my goods are here. They were brought back at three o'clock."

"By Lupin?"

"By two army-wagons."

Sherlock Holmes put on his cap and adjusted his satchel. Devanne exclaimed, anxiously:

"But, monsieur, what are you going to do?"

"I am going home."

"Why?"

"Your goods have been returned; Arsène Lupin in far away—there is nothing for me to do."

"Yes, there is. I need your assistance. What happened yesterday, may happen again to-morrow, as we do not know how he entered, or how he escaped, or why, a few hours later, he returned the goods."

"Ah! you don't know—"

The idea of a problem to be solved quickened the interest of Sherlock Holmes.

"Very well, let us make a search—at once —and alone, if possible."

Devanne understood, and conducted the Englishman to the salon. In a dry, crisp voice, in sentences that seemed to have been prepared in advance, Holmes asked a number of questions about the events of the preceding evening, and enquired also concerning the guests and the members of the household. Then he examined the two volumes of the "Chronique," compared the plans of the subterranean passage, requested a repetition of the sentences discovered by Father Gélis, and then asked:

"Was yesterday the first time you have spoken of those two sentences to any one?"

"Yes."

"You had never communicated then to Horace Velmont?"

"No."

"Well, order the automobile. I must leave in an hour."

"In an hour?"

"Yes; within that time, Arsène Lupin solved the problem that you placed before him."

"I....I placed before him—"

"Yes, Arsène Lupin or Horace Velmont—same thing."

"I thought so. Ah! the scoundrel!"

"Now, let us see," said Holmes, "last night at ten o'clock, you furnished Lupin

with the information that he lacked, and that
he had been seeking for many weeks. During
the night, he found time to solve the problem, collect his men, and rob the castle. I
shall be quite as expeditious.''

He walked from end to end of the room, in
deep thought, then sat down, crossed his long
legs and closed his eyes.

Devanne waited, quite embarrassed.
Thought he: ''Is the man asleep? Or is he
only meditating?'' However, he left the
room to give some orders, and when he returned he found the detective on his knees
scrutinizing the carpet at the foot of the
stairs in the gallery.

''What it is?'' he enquired.

''What is it?'' he enquired.

''Look....there....spots from a candle.''

''You are right—and quite fresh.''

''And you will also find them at the top of
the stairs, and around the cabinet that Arsène
Lupin broke into, and from which he took the
bibelots that he afterward placed in this armchair.''

''What do you conclude from that?''

''Nothing. These facts would doubtless
explain the cause for the restitution, but that
is a side issue that I cannot wait to investi-

gate. The main question is the secret passage. First, tell me, is there a chapel some two or three hundred metres from the castle?"

"Yes, a ruined chapel, containing the tomb of Duke Rollo."

"Tell your chauffeur to wait for us near that chapel."

"My chauffeur hasn't returned. If he had, they would have informed me. Do you think the secret passage runs to the chapel? What reason have—"

"I would ask you, monsieur," interrupted the detective, "to furnish me with a ladder and a lantern."

"What! do you require a ladder and a lantern?"

"Certainly, or I shouldn't have asked for them."

Devanne, somewhat disconcerted by this crude logic, rang the bell. The two articles were brought. The succeeding orders were given with the sternness and precision of military commands.

"Place the ladder against the bookcase, to the left of the word Thibermesnil."

Devanne placed the ladder as directed, and the Englishman continued:

"More to the left....to the right....
There!.... Now, climb up.... All the
letters are in relief, aren't they?"

"Yes."

"First, turn the letter I one way or the
other."

"Which one? There are two of them."

"The first one."

Devanne took hold of the letter, and
exclaimed:

"Ah! yes, it turns toward the right. Who
told you that?"

Sherlock Holmes did not reply to the question, but continued his directions:

"Now, take the letter B. Move it back
and forth as you would a bolt."

Devanne did so, and, to his great surprise,
it produced a clicking sound.

"Quite right," said Holmes. "Now, we
will go to the other end of the word Thibermesnil, try the letter I, and see if it will open
like a wicket."

With a certain degree of solemnity,
Devanne seized the letter. It opened, but
Devanne fell from the ladder, for the entire
section of the bookcase, lying between the
first and last letters of the words, turned on

a pivot and disclosed the subterranean passage.

Sherlock Holmes said, coolly:

"You are not hurt?"

"No, no," said Devanne, as he rose to his feet, "not hurt, only bewildered. I can't understand now....those letters turn....the secret passage opens...."

"Certainly. Doesn't that agree exactly with the formula given by Sully? Turn one eye on the bee that shakes, the other eye will lead to God."

"But Louis the sixteenth?" asked Devanne.

"Louis the sixteenth was a clever locksmith. I have read a book he wrote about combination locks. It was a good idea on the part of the owner of Thibermesnil to show to His Majesty a clever bit of mechanism. As an aid to his memory, the king wrote: 3—4—11, that is to say, the third, fourth and eleventh letters of the word."

"Exactly. I understand that. It explains how Lupin got out of the room, but it does not explain how he entered. And it is certain he came from the outside."

Sherlock Holmes lighted his lantern, and stepped into the passage.

"Look! All the mechanism is exposed

here, like the works of a clock, and the reverse
side of the letters can be reached. Lupin
worked the combination from this side—that
is all.''

''What proof is there of that?''

''Proof? Why, look at that puddle of oil.
Lupin foresaw even that the wheels would
require oiling.''

''Did he know about the other entrance?''

''As well as I know it,'' said Holmes.
''Follow me.''

''Into that dark passage?''

''Are you afraid?''

''No, but are you sure you can find the
way out?''

''With my eyes closed.''

At first, they descended twelve steps, then
twelve more, and, farther on, two other flights
of twelve steps each. Then they walked
through a long passageway, the brick walls
of which showed the marks of successive res-
torations, and, in spots, were dripping with
water. The earth, also, was very damp.

''We are passing under the pond,'' said
Devanne, somewhat nervously.

At last, they came to a stairway of twelve
steps, followed by three others of twelve

steps each, which they mounted with difficulty, and then found themselves in a small
cavity cut in the rock. They could go no
farther.

"The deuce!" muttered Holmes, "nothing
but bare walls. This is provoking."

"Let us go back," said Devanne. "I have
seen enough to satisfy me."

But the Englishman raised his eyes and
uttered a sigh of relief. There, he saw the
same mechanism and the same word as before. He had merely to work the three
letters. He did so, and a block of granite
swung out of place. On the other side, this
granite block formed the tombstone of Duke
Rollo, and the word "Thibermesnil" was
engraved on it in relief. Now, they were in
the little ruined chapel, and the detective
said:

"The other eye leads to God; that means,
to the chapel."

"It is marvellous!" exclaimed Devanne,
amazed at the clairvoyance and vivacity of
the Englishman. "Can it be possible that
those few words were sufficient for you?"

"Bah!" declared Holmes, "they weren't
even necessary. In the chart in the book of

the National Library, the drawing terminates
at the left, as you know, in a circle, and at
the right, as you do not know, in a cross.
Now, that cross must refer to the chapel in
which we now stand.''

Poor Devanne could not believe his ears.
It was all so new, so novel to him. He
exclaimed:

"It is incredible, miraculous, and yet of a
childish simplicity! How is it that no one
has ever solved the mystery?''

"Because no one has ever united the essential elements, that is to say, the two books
and the two sentences. No one, but Arsène
Lupin and myself.''

"But, Father Gélis and I knew all about
those things, and, likewise—''

Holmes smiled, and said:

"Monsieur Devanne, everybody cannot
solve riddles.''

"I have been trying for ten years to accomplish what you did in ten minutes.''

"Bah! I am used to it.''

They emerged from the chapel, and found
an automobile.

"Ah! there's an auto waiting for us.''

"Yes, it is mine,'' said Devanne.

"Yours? You said your chauffeur hadn't returned."

They approached the machine, and Mon. Devanne questioned the chauffeur:

"Edouard, who gave you orders to come here?"

"Why, it was Monsieur Velmont."

"Mon. Velmont? Did you meet him?"

"Near the railway station, and he told me to come to the chapel."

"To come to the chapel! What for?"

"To wait for you, monsieur, and your friend."

Devanne and Holmes exchanged looks, and Mon. Devanne said:

"He knew the mystery would be a simple one for you. It is a delicate compliment."

A smile of satisfaction lighted up the detective's serious features for a moment. The compliment pleased him. He shook his head, as he said:

"A clever man! I knew that when I saw him."

"Have you seen him?"

"I met him a short time ago—on my way from the station."

"And you knew it was Horace Velmont— I mean, Arsène Lupin?"

"That is right. I wonder how it came—"

"No, but I supposed it was—from a certain ironical speech he made."

"And you allowed him to escape?"

"Of course I did. And yet I had everything on my side, such as five gendarmes who passed us."

"Sacrableu!" cried Devanne. "You should have taken advantage of the opportunity."

"Really, monsieur," said the Englishman, haughtily, "when I encounter an adversary like Arsène Lupin, I do not take advantage of chance opportunities, I create them."

But time pressed, and since Lupin had been so kind as to send the automobile, they resolved to profit by it. They seated themselves in the comfortable limousine; Edouard took his place at the wheel, and away they went toward the railway station. Suddenly, Devanne's eyes fell upon a small package in one of the pockets of the carriage.

"Ah! what is that? A package! Whose is it? Why, it is for you."

"For me?"

"Yes, it is addressed: Sherlock Holmes, from Arsène Lupin."

The Englishman took the package, opened it, and found that it contained a watch.

"Ah!" he exclaimed, with an angry gesture.

"A watch," said Devanne. "How did it come there?"

The detective did not reply.

"Oh! it is your watch! Arsène Lupin returns your watch! But, in order to return it, he must have taken it. Ah! I see! He took your watch! That is a good one! Sherlock Holmes' watch stolen by Arsène Lupin! Mon Dieu! that is funny! Really....you must excuse me.... I can't help it."

He roared with laughter, unable to control himself. After which, he said, in a tone of earnest conviction:

"A clever man, indeed!"

The Englishman never moved a muscle. On the way to Dieppe, he never spoke a word, but fixed his gaze on the flying landscape. His silence was terrible, unfathomable, more violent than the wildest rage. At the railway station, he spoke calmly, but in a voice that impressed one with the vast energy and will power of that famous man. He said:

"Yes, he is a clever man, but some day I shall have the pleasure of placing on his shoulder the hand I now offer to you, Mon-

sieur Devanne. And I believe that Arsène
Lupin and Sherlock Holmes will meet again
some day. Yes, the world is too small—we
will meet—we must meet—and then—"

*The further startling and thrilling adven-
tures of Arsène Lupin will be found in the
book entitled "Arsène Lupin versus Herlock
Sholmes."*

*For sale by all booksellers or sent to any
address upon receipt of 75c by*

*M. A. DONOHUE & CO., Publishers
Chicago*

9 781162 722276